Bead Embroidery Stitch Samples
Motifs

Embroidery, Crewel, Cross Stitch, Mini Motifs and More!

YASUKO ENDO & CRK DESIGN

 INTERWEAVE

Bead Embroidery Stitch Samples
by CRK design / Yasuko Endo

First designed and published in Japan in 2011
by Graphic-sha Publishing Co., Ltd.
1-14-17 Kudan-kita, Chiyoda-ku,
Tokyo 102-0073 Japan

English language edition published in 2014
by Interweave

First published in the United States of America by
Interweave, a division of F+W Media, Inc.
201 East Fourth Street
Loveland, CO 80537-5655
www.interweave.com

ISBN 978-1-62033-610-6

10 9 8 7 6 5 4 3 2 1

Library of Congress Cataloging-in-Publication Data
Yasuko Endo/ CRK design
Bead Embroidery Stitch Samples by CRK design/Yasuko Endo
pages cm
Summary: "Combine your love for hand stitching with beautiful beads to make delightfully original trims and embellishments" - Provided by publisher.
Includes bibliographical references and index.
ISBN 978-1-62033-610-6
1. Crafts-Jewelry 2. Beadwork - Patterns
Title. III Title: Bead Embroidery Stitch Samples: Motifs

Planning, production, editing & book design:	Chiaki Kitaya, Yasuko Endo and Kuma Imamura (CRK design)
Stitch design & piece production:	Yasuko Endo (CRK design)
Alphabet design:	Kaoru Emoto (CRK design)
Cooperation to piece production:	Midori Nishida, Setsuko Ishii, Takako Nogi and Yoko Ogawa
Photography:	Yoshiharu Ohtaki (studio seek)
Procedure photography:	Nobuei Araki (studio seek)
Styling:	CRK design
Model:	Masumi Minato
Editing and illustration for Lesson Note pages:	Kuma Imamura (CRK design)
Cooperation to editing & illustrations:	Tomoko Kajiyama
Cooperation to photo shooting:	AWABEES

English edition
Layout:	Shinichi Ishioka
Translation:	Sean Gaston, Yuko Wada, Takako Otomo
Editing and production:	Kumiko Sakamoto (Graphic-sha Publishing Co., Ltd.)

Printed and bound in China

CONTENTS

BASIC LESSON

MINI MOTIF

CREWEL

BASIC STITCHES

CROSS STITCHES

MINI MOTIF

LESSON NOTES

Materials & Tools
Basics of Embroidery
Sweet Motifs with Bead Embroidery Stitches

BASIC LESSON

For more information about shortcakes and the stitches, see page 68.

For the number of each stitch and materials, see page 88.

Materials & Tools

Beads

Round Beads (3.0mm, 8/0) / (3-5mm, 1/8"-1/5")

The most popular round bead. With a slightly large hole, a feature of TOHO Beads, it is suitable for embroidery thread, as it is easy to insert a needle into the hole. The beads offer a variety of textures through various processing types such as clear, matte, aurora and plate.

Bugle Beads

Long cylinder-type beads. The most commonly used one in the series is the 3mm-long bugle bead. 6mm-long and 9mm-long bugle beads are also available. You can enjoy many choices of length for your design.

TOHO Beads

Crewel Wool Embroidery Thread

Wool Embroidery Thread

Pure wool embroidery thread consists of slender threads twisted together a little loosely. With this thread, you can enjoy embroidery finished warmly and gently with a fluffy texture. You can also enjoy diversified combinations between beads and colors with the wide selection of thread colors from vivid to subtle. About 20 meters per bundle

Beads DMC Embroidery Thread

Embroidery Thread No.25

With the wide selection of thread colors available, you can enjoy unlimited options for color matching. This book shows pieces using beautiful space dyes such as "ombre" and "color variation". This thread is difficult to become discolored by water or sunlight, keeping its beauty for a long time.

Embroidery Thread No.5

The cotton pearl series of embroidery thread with a soft texture like silk, and shines like pearl. The thickish thread twisted together loosely is suitable for voluminous embroidery or woven-like stitches.

Diamant

Metallic embroidery thread with an attractive and elegant diamond-like shine. The thread is much smoother than traditional lamé thread, and has resistance to friction, offering a beautiful finish. It's also easy to thread, as the twist is difficult to become untwisted. It's useful for not only embroidery but also any needlework.

Fabrics

While embroidery can be made on any fabric, special fabrics for embroidery are used for pieces in this book. They allow you to count and align stitches easily, as the texture of linen and cotton are regular.
Embroidery can also be accomplished smoothly with these fabrics, as they are easy to insert a needle and are resilient. (Fabrics are sorted by the number of threads per centimeter.)

DMC Printed Needle Work Fabrics

14-count stripe print. Pink x White & Blue x White

DMC Needle Work Fabrics

High-quality linen for embroidery. 28-count and 32-count types are available.

Waste Canvas

Useful for doing a counted cross-stitch on a fabric where the grain can't be counted. After stitching, mist it with water and remove it. For instructions on how to use, see page 11.

Fusible Interfacing for Embroidery

Useful when you stitch on stretchy fabric such as knits. Iron it onto the reverse side of the fabric to temporarily stabilize and make it easier to stitch. For instructions on how to use, see page 11.

Needles

Embroidery Needles

They are recommended for embroidery with beads. The needle tip is pointed and it goes through fabric smoothly. An "Assortment pack" is useful because you can use the best needle depending on the gauge and number of yarn threads used. Please refer to page 9 for the correspondence table with beads and embroidery threads.

Embroidery Hoops

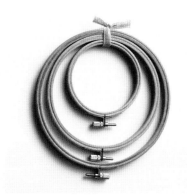

Embroidery hoops

They make a thin and loose fabric easier to cross-stitch by stretching it tight with the hoop. Use it carefully to avoid damage to the fabric and beads, referring to page 10.

Marking & Rulers

Use a paper chalk (one side type) which comes out with water to transfer a pattern. To draw guidelines, use a water-soluble marker (with eraser) with which you can erase any part quickly. For rulers, must-have tools, a plotting scale that is easy to check even on a dark color fabric or fabric with dark-colored patterns is recommended.

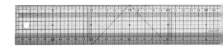

Basics of Embroidery Before getting started…

Threads   Tip on handling threads: Wash your hands well in advance.

Made by twisting together 6 slender threads. Pull the desired number of slender threads to control its thickness. For example, a "double yarn" refers to a thread made by bundling together two of these threads.

In this book, a needle thinner than usual may be used to thread beads.

1 Pull out the thread #25 and cut it into a 45-50 cm (17 3/4" - 19 3/4") length. If it is too long, the thread may fray or spoil easily.

2 Pull out the required number of slender threads one by one. Even if using it as a sextuple yarn, remove all one by one and re-bundle them.

3 Bundle together the required number of slender threads, aligning the ends.

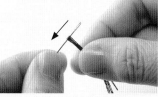

4 Fold the bundled thread over a needle and pull the needle in the direction of the arrow, holding the thread firmly.

5 Insert the folded part of the thread into the needle hole.

6 Pull one end of the thread through and keep the length of the shorter thread about 10 cm (4").

Embroidery thread #5

A loop of a bundled single long thick thread. Cut thread to a length easy for use later.

1 Remove the labels and loosen the loop of twisted thread bundle.

2 Cut the knot part tying the thread together.

A label with the color number.

3 Thread the label with the bundle again and tie it loosely into a braid. Pull out thread from the folded part one by one for use in embroidery.

Beads   Tips on handling beads: Separate packed loose beads by type. Do not use beads that require force to insert a needle into the hole.

Recommended combination of beads, needles and threads

The following table shows the type of thread, and size of needles suited for given beads. But if you already have needles suitable for the threads and beads you need, go ahead and use them. For stretchy knit fabrics in T-shirts and the like, a needle with a round point is recommended to make stitching smooth, as it is hard to get stuck in the fabric. An embroidery needle instead of a cross-stitch needle is used for cross-stitches in this book, as it uses round beads.

Needle		Embroidery needle	Beads
Embroidery needle	No.9	Embroidery thread No.25 (double-triple yarns)	Round bead (3-5mm, 1/8"-1/5")/bugle bead
	No.8	Embroidery thread No.25 (double-triple yarns)	Round bead (3-5mm, 1/8"-1/5")/bugle bead
	No.7	Embroidery thread No.25 (double-quadruple yarns) & No.5	Round bead 8/0 (3.0mm)
	No.6	Embroidery thread No.25 (triple-quadruple yarns), No.5 & cruel wool	Round bead 8/0 (3.0mm)
Beads embroidery needle/ sewing needle		Sewing yarn	Round bead (3-5mm, 1/8"-1/5")/ Round bead 8/0 (3.0mm)

Separate and keep beads in a small containers by type. This is useful when you would like to use a small amount.

Basics of Embroidery How to use tools & tips to make the work more fun.

Mark & Trace

Tip : Marking, tracing and other tools used differ depending on the pattern or embroidery fabric.

Marking with dots and lines

Lines and dots can be used as a guide showing the width or interval of stitches.

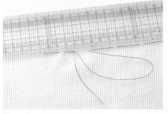

Water-soluble marker (with eraser)
For normal fabric such as cotton or linen. You can erase any part quickly with water or the accompanying eraser.

Pencil-type chalk
Useful for marking up even dark color fabric. It comes out easily with your fingers or the accompanying brush.

Threads
For fabric on which markers, including pencil-type chalks, are unusable, mark by sewing with thread such as a sewing yarn.

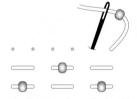

To align the width of stitches exactly, draw solid lines.

To make the intervals precisely uniform, mark with dots to guide points to insert a needle.

To make stitch shapes uniform, trace the pattern accurately.

Trace patterns

To trace the shape of stitches precisely, use a paper chalk (one sided type). Trace patterns, fixing the paper chalk firmly with pins or tape.

① Trace patterns on thin paper such as a tracing paper.

② Apply the transferable side to the fabric and lay the traced patterns on it. Place cellophane on this to smooth the surface and copy the patterns on with a tracer.

③ After tracing, check to ensure important patterns such as flower petals are traced fully, and you can determine points to insert a needle for regular and repeating motifs.

Embroidery Hoop

Tip on handling hoops: When working on small patterns or stable fabrics, it is enough to stretch the fabric with your fingers without using this tool.

Setting up a tambour

This hoop is useful when using thin or loose fabric, or embroidery involving counting the number of grains, such as cross-stitches.

① To protect and fix an embroidery fabric, wrap a bias-cut fabric around the inner hoop.

② Encase fabric on the inner hoop in the outer hoop, fixing by screwing it down. Cover the beaded part on the hoop with another fabric, fixing loosely to the outer hoop.

③ Pull the fabric along the grain evenly to make it easier to insert the needle. Then be careful not to distort the grain.

Technique 1

Do a counted cross-stitch on any fabric. : You can stitch in the normal way on a fabric which has a grain that is difficult to count.

Waste canvas

Tack it temporarily to a fabric to make it easier to count the grain. After stitching, remove the waste canvas yarn.
*This is useful for cross-stitch, Holbein stitch, herringbone stitch, zigzag stitch, etc.

1 Cut waste canvas to a size slightly larger than the pattern, and tack it to the fabric.

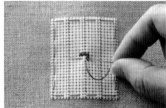
2 Make cross-stitches. Draw the thread a little tight because the waste canvas will be removed later.

3 Stitch a letter. Remove stitches tacking the canvas temporarily.

4 Mist the whole area with water to melt away the starch of the waste canvas.

5 Remove the weaving yarn of the waste canvas one by one.

6 Complete.

Technique 2

Stitching on knits : Put fusible interfacing or Japanese paper on a soft and stretchy fabric.

Affix fusible interfacing

Using an iron at low heat, temporarily affix fusible interfacing to a fabric to reinforce. You can also tack with Japanese paper.

1 Cut fusible interfacing to a size slightly larger than the pattern, and affix it to the fabric temporarily using an iron at low heat.

2 After stitching, tear and remove the fusible interfacing carefully. Take care not to pull the thread.

3 The thread is not too loose or tight.

Technique 3

When running out of thread. : Continue with new thread to avoid any strange gaps in the pattern.

Join threads in the middle of stitching

When you do stitches which require wrapping thread around needle, for example chain stitch or fly stitch, allow leeway at the thread end and join a new thread linking patterns to adjust the shape.

1 Stitch the last stitch loosely and leave the thread end on the back without a knot.

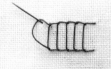
2 Pass a new thread through the needle, inserting the needle from the back and wrapping the thread of the last stitch around the needle.

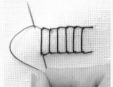
3 Make the next stitch, pulling the thread from the back to adjust the stitch, taking care of the thread end.

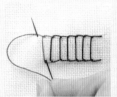
4 Continue stitching the pattern with the new thread.

Sweet Motifs with Bead Embroidery Stitches

Cute and natural striped T-shirt and half pants for kids

A small sweet motif of beads and embroidery threads can be an easy first design. Let's eat a donut made from couching stitches together with a fork of bugle beads!

Material
- T-shirt and half pants
- Embroidery thread: DMC #25/No. 605 (pink), No. 436 (dark beige), BLANC (white)
- Bead: TOHO round bead 11/0 (2.2mm) No. 332 (red-purple), No. 931 (blue), No. 121 (white)/3mm-long bugle bead No. 121 (white)
- Linen cloth (Linen cloth for embroidery is firm and easy to stitch even without a hoop.)
- Needle: Clover embroidery needle (No.9)
- Water-soluble marker (with eraser), scale, scissors, fray stopper

Mark up fabric
Refer to the illustration on the left to mark up fabric, and draw freehand a donut ring.

Tools
Even if the line sticks out, you can correct it at once with a very useful marker with eraser.

Life-sized pattern

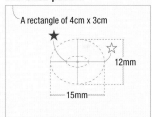

A rectangle of 4cm x 3cm
12mm
15mm

Preparation of embroidery threads

Cut the embroidery threads of #25 into lengths of about 50cm (19 5/8") and draw out the necessary number of threads as shown below in Figs. A and B. A fine embroidery needle is used so that it can pass through small round beads. Without folding the thread, bring the ends of the threads together tightly, then squeeze the end into the hole of the needle, pushing it in with your fingertips.

Hold the end of the thread with the needle and wrap the thread around the needle a couple of times. Hold the wrapped part tightly with a fingertip and draw out the needle.

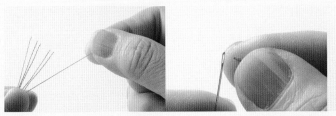

A: Core thread (triple yarn)

B: Fixing thread (double yarn)

Tip Make sure to draw out the threads one by one. They may get tangled if you draw out multiple threads.

Start! Lay the core thread along the inner circle and fix it with another thread.

   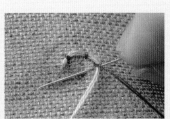

1. Bring the needle with thread A (core thread) up from the back, on the line of the inner circle (★ on the pattern).

2. Bring the needle with thread B (fixing thread) up from the back, on the point a little way away along the line of the circle.
*Thread B is different color to make it easy to understand.

3. Lay thread A along the circle and fix it with thread B. Refer to the pattern for the fixing points. Bring the needle with thread B up from the back to the position you want to fix thread A to next.

4. Fix thread A at regular intervals in the same way to draw a circle with thread A along the inner circle.

Embroidery threads/beads used

A. Embroidery thread #25/No. 164 (light green), No. 433 (brown),
   BLANC (white)/round bead 11/0 (2.2mm) No. 329 (brown), No.
   405 (red)/3mm-long bugle bead No. 121 (white)

B. Embroidery thread #25/No. 433 (brown), No. 437 (beige), BLANC
   (white)/round bead 11/0 (2.2mm) No. 175 (yellow), No. 185 (red),
   No. 931 (blue)/3mm-long bugle bead No. 121 (white)

C. Embroidery thread #25/BLANC (white), No. 435 (dark beige)/
   round bead 11/0 (2.2mm) No. 332 (red-purple), No. 111 (orange),
   No. 175 (yellow)/3mm-long bugle bead No. 43 (aqua)

A Bittersweet green tea
donut

B Soft donut with
chocolate frosting

C Old-fashioned donut
with white chocolate

5 When you make a full circle, bring
the needle with thread B up from the
back at the starting point of thread
A, and fix thread A with thread B,
hiding the starting point.

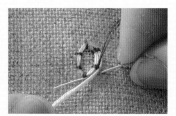

6 Lay thread A along the 1st circle to
make a 2nd circle, and fix it at the
same points as the 1st circle.

7 After going half way around of the
3rd circle, take 6 beads and set them
one by one in between the fixing
points.

8 After going half way around the 4th
circle, 6 beads are placed at regular
intervals. Then make another full
circle with thread A without beads.

9 Pass the needle with thread A in the
fabric at the side of the outer circle
(☆ on the pattern on page 6). Fix
thread A with thread B hiding the
end.

Topping completed!

Tip Make a knot after passing the thread to the back,
and then cut it after lacing it through the stitched
threads.

Donut completed!

10 Pass the needle with thread A to
make a donut motif from the back
at the ending point of the topping
motif. Pass the needle with thread
B at the point in between the fixing
points of the topping motif.

11 Fix thread A along the topping motif
to make a donut motif. After going
half way round, fold it back carefully
to return to the starting point.

12 Finish the end of the thread in the
same way as the topping motif and
your donut motif is complete!

13 Draft the position of the fork with a marker considering the alignment.

14 Make the shape of fork tines with a fly stitch, and make another stitch with a 3mm-long bugle bead and a round bead to form a handle.

15 Push the bead with a needle to adjust the shape, and pass the needle at the position of the bead.

16 Make a straight stitch in between the stitch forming the fork tines and the fork motif is complete.

Tip

Be careful not to pull the thread too tight in making a fly stitch (left) or to spread the first stitch too much (right).

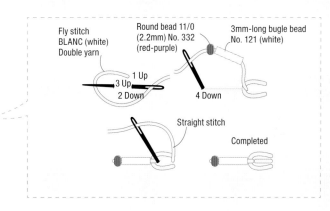

Fly stitch BLANC (white) Double yarn
Round bead 11/0 (2.2mm) No. 332 (red-purple)
3mm-long bugle bead No. 121 (white)
1 Up
3 Up
2 Down
4 Down
Straight stitch
Completed

17 Cut out the fabric taking care to keep the donut in the center.

18 Put a fray stopper on the cut edge of the fabric and dry it. Note that too much fray stopper may discolor the fabric.

19 Place the motifs on a T-shirt to decide on the positioning and mark with a water-soluble marker.

20 Fix the center motif with a running stitch, threading a bead every other stitch. In the same way, fix the right and left motifs, checking the alignment.

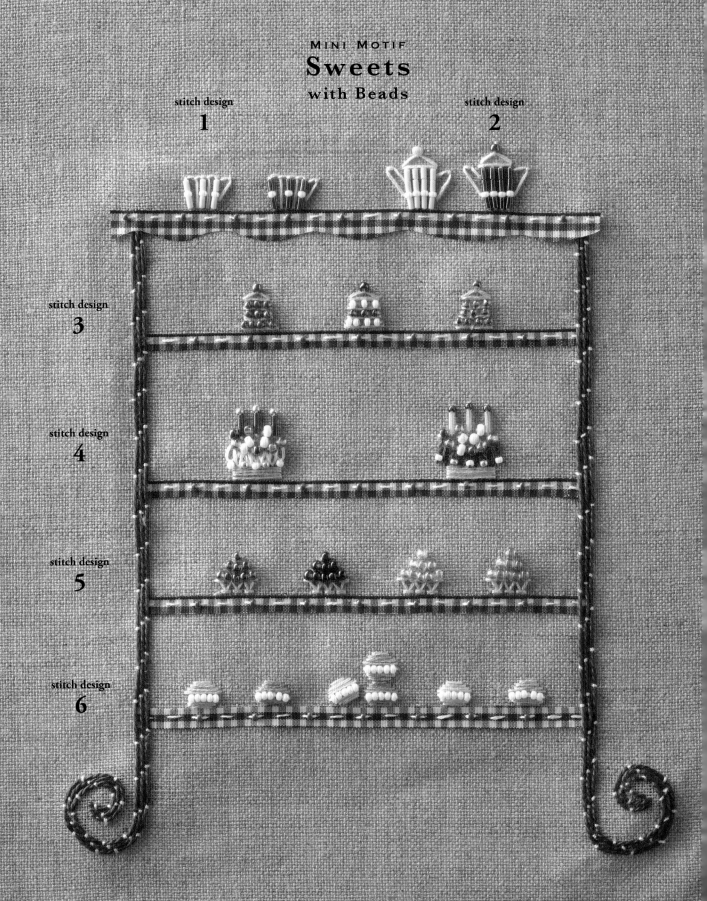

MINI MOTIF
Sweets
with Beads

stitch design
1

stitch design
2

stitch design
3

stitch design
4

stitch design
5

stitch design
6

Adding beads to sweets motif...

1   Insert a bead every other blanket stitch to make a cup.

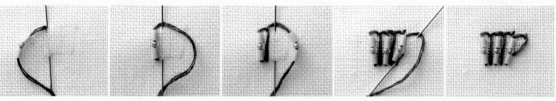

2   Stitch a cover with a fly stitch to make a pot to match with the cup above.

3   Using beads to resemble fruit, stitch them one by one evenly to make a pancake.

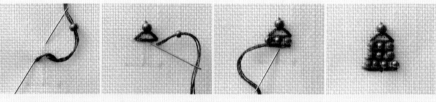

4   Decorate a birthday frosting with cream made of fly stitches and beads, and put candles of bugle beads on top of it.

5   Make a tart of chevron stitches, using beads to resemble fruits.

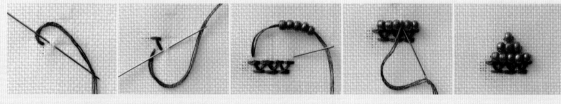

6   Create a filling of beads in straight stitches...a lovely macaroon is made.

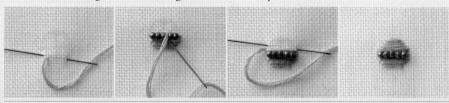

For the display shelf for sweets pattern, refer to page 67.

Sweets Motif with Beads (1-6)

MINI MOTIF

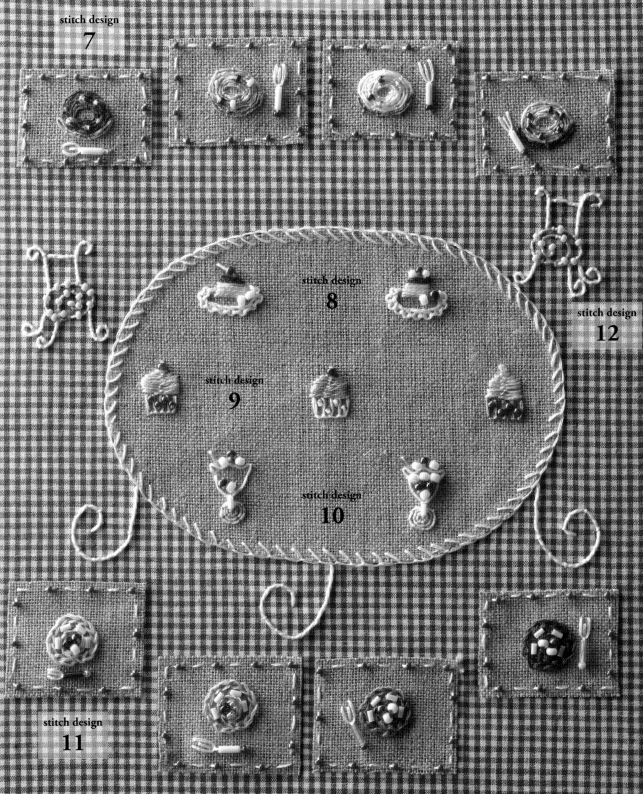

stitch design
7

stitch design
8

stitch design
12

stitch design
9

stitch design
10

stitch design
11

Adding beads to a sweets motif...

7 Make a couple of circles with couching stitches adding beads to form a donut. Change the color of threads to create a topping of chocolate, strawberry or green tea icing.

Sweets Motif

When you pick up the basic stitches to make the sweets motif, why not decorate your favorite sweets with fruits and frosting made of beads?

Sweets with Beads (1-6)

8 To make a pudding motif, stitch in a trapezoidal shape. Make a dish with Pekinese stitches to complete the motif.

9 Frost a cupcake with Romanian stitches. The trick is to stitch in a fluffy round shape.

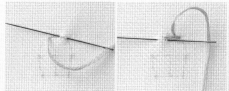

10 Make an outline of a parfait glass with couching stitches, and add fruit of round beads and a straw of bugle bead.

11 You can stitch in a circle with small chain stitches. Change the color of the cake roll, icing and fruits as you like.

12 Make a chair with couching stitches adding beads.

For the table pattern, refer to page 67.

MINI MOTIF

Sweets Motif with Beads (7-12)

MINI MOTIF
Ethnic Costumes
with Beads

stitch design
13

Finland

stitch design
14

stitch design
15

stitch design
16

Sweden

stitch design
17

stitch design
18

stitch design
19

Estonia

stitch design
20

stitch design
21

stitch design
22

Hungary

stitch design
23

stitch design
24

stitch design
25

Swiss

stitch design
26

stitch design
27

14 Stitch using a unique Lapland costume as a motif.

18 Use pink and white beads to resemble an apron.

20 A sash is represented with red bugle beads, in the style of the Russia Cossack.

23 A scarf around the waist is made with red beads.

26 Green beads project a Swiss image.

Adding beads to an ethnic costume...

15 Add a cap and boots of red beads for cold weather.

17 Elongate the skirt of a jacket to make a formal impression.

21 Round beads represent bouffant sleeves, and the red veil on the head is made with fly stitches.

24 A colorful apron and skirt are intentionally short to emphasize the boots.

27 Bugle beads represent a white apron to coordinate with a red skirt.

Ethnic Motif with Beads (13-27)

MINI MOTIF

MINI MOTIF
Ethnic Costumes
with Beads

stitch design
28

French

stitch design **29**   stitch design **30**

stitch design
31

Greece

stitch design **32**   stitch design **33**

stitch design
34

Turkey

stitch design **35**   stitch design **36**

stitch design
37

Mexico

stitch design **38**   stitch design **39**

stitch design
40

Peru

stitch design **41**   stitch design **42**

29 A sash of red beads is an eye-catching point.

32 A short pleated skirt, this Greek ethnic costume, is made with straight stitches.

35 Stitch a long tunic and add a turban.

39 Aqua and black beads represent a clear print dress.

42 Put a colorful poncho around the shoulders, and make braids with small round beads.

Adding beads to an ethnic costume...

30 A headdress unique to Alsace is represented by round beads.

33 Stitch bugle beads spreading them toward the bottom to resemble a fluffy skirt.

36 A pair of harem pants is made with loose Double Lazy Daisy stitches, and a veil of the same color is added.

38 A sombrero and a red sash are eye-catching.

41 Put a short poncho and a black hat on the motif.

21

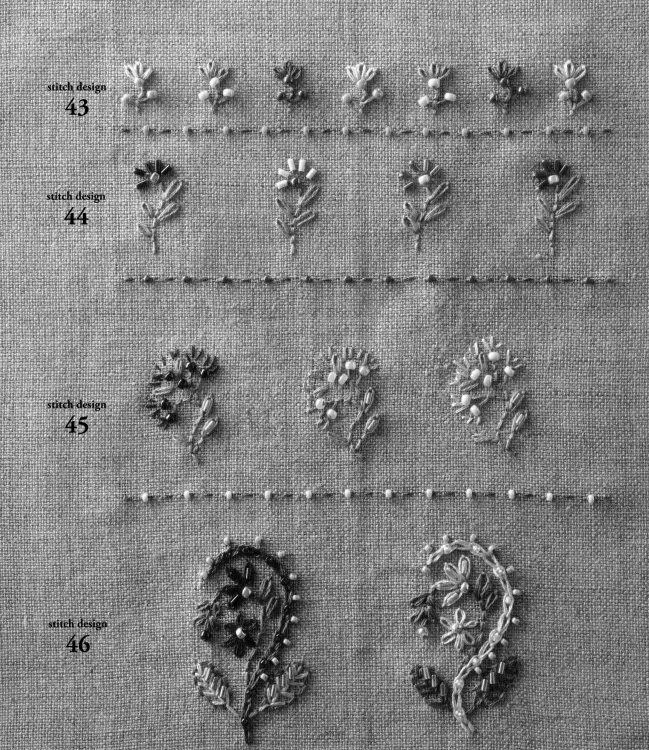

stitch design
43

stitch design
44

stitch design
45

stitch design
46

Decorate a paisley motif with beads

43 Stitch a bead as the center of the flower at a slight angle to show fluidity.

44 Curve the stem to show the movement of the flower.

45 Use the same type of color for the center and the petals of the flowers.

46 Make a paisley motif with petals and leaves of Lazy Daisy stitches, accompanying chain stitches to them. Add beads as a decorative accent.

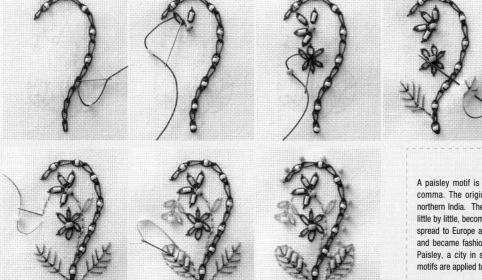

Paisley

A paisley motif is a pattern in the shape of a dewdrop similar to a comma. The origin of the pattern is a floral pattern in Kashmir of northern India. The floral pattern incorporated "fluidity" and developed little by little, becoming stylized. In the 18th century, Indian dyed fabrics spread to Europe and surrounding areas, and the paisley motif spread and became fashionable after production of Kashmir shawls began in Paisley, a city in southwestern Scotland. Presently, various paisley motifs are applied to printed fabrics.

MINI MOTIF

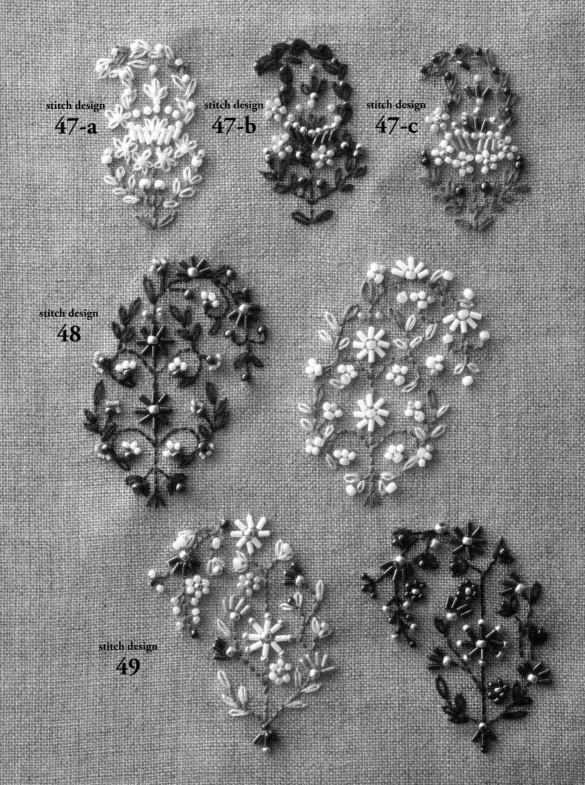

stitch design
47-a

stitch design
47-b

stitch design
47-c

stitch design
48

stitch design
49

Decorate a paisley motif with beads...

47-c Make a bouquet in the shape of paisley with flowers of beads and leaves of Lazy Daisy stitches.

48 Make a paisley motif with backstitches and Lazy Daisy stitches. Bead flowers are very eye-catching.

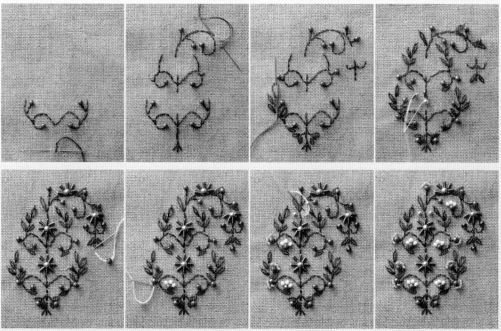

MINI MOTIF

43 Life-size pattern

❶ Copy the pattern.

❷ Stitch petals with Lazy Daisy stitches. Stitch the center petal first and then stitch the right and left petals in a balanced manner.

❸ Fix a round bead 8/0 (3.0mm) as the center of the flower in the same manner as a back stitch.

❹ Then make a stem with back stitches.

❺ Fix beads to the right and left of the stem in the same manner as a back stitch.

Completed
*All embroidery threads are triple yarn.

No. 3328 (dark pink)   No. 3821 (yellow)   No. 3733 (pink)
No. 405 (red)   No. 407 (green)   No. 403 (aqua)
No. 3347 (grass green)   No. 519 (aqua)   No. 3347 (grass green)

Embroidery threads/beads used

Embroidery thread: DMC #25/No. 3347 (grass green), No. 3328 (dark pink), No. 3821 (yellow), No. 519 (aqua), No. 3733 (pink)
Bead: TOHO round bead 8/0 (3.0mm) No. 405 (red), No. 407 (green), No. 403 (aqua)

44 Life-size pattern

❶ Copy the pattern.

❷ Fix a round bead 8/0 (3.0mm) as the center of the flower.

❸ Fix 3mm-long bugle beads radially in the same manner as straight stitches.

❹ Make a stem with back stitches.

❺ Make leaves with Lazy Daisy stitches.

Embroidery threads/beads used

Embroidery thread: DMC #25/No. 988 (green)
Bead: TOHO round bead 8/0 (3.0mm) No. 557 (gold), No. 405 (red), No. 403 (aqua), No. 905 (pink)/3mm-long bugle bead No. 332 (red-purple), No. 43 (aqua), No. 165 (red), No. 45 (red)

Completed
*All embroidery threads are triple yarn.

No. 332 (red-purple)   No. 43 (aqua)   No 165 (red)   No. 45 (red)
No. 557 (gold)   No. 405 (red)   No. 403 (aqua)   No. 905 (pink)
No. 988 (green)   No. 988 (green)   No. 988 (green)   No. 988 (green)

45 Life-size pattern

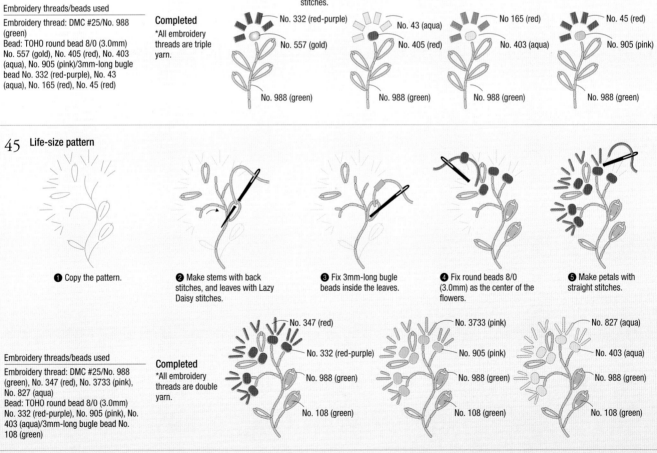

❶ Copy the pattern.

❷ Make stems with back stitches, and leaves with Lazy Daisy stitches.

❸ Fix 3mm-long bugle beads inside the leaves.

❹ Fix round beads 8/0 (3.0mm) as the center of the flowers.

❺ Make petals with straight stitches.

Embroidery threads/beads used

Embroidery thread: DMC #25/No. 988 (green), No. 347 (red), No. 3733 (pink), No. 827 (aqua)
Bead: TOHO round bead 8/0 (3.0mm) No. 332 (red-purple), No. 905 (pink), No. 403 (aqua)/3mm-long bugle bead No. 108 (green)

Completed
*All embroidery threads are double yarn.

No. 347 (red)   No. 3733 (pink)   No. 827 (aqua)
No. 332 (red-purple)   No. 905 (pink)   No. 403 (aqua)
No. 988 (green)   No. 988 (green)   No. 988 (green)
No. 108 (green)   No. 108 (green)   No. 108 (green)

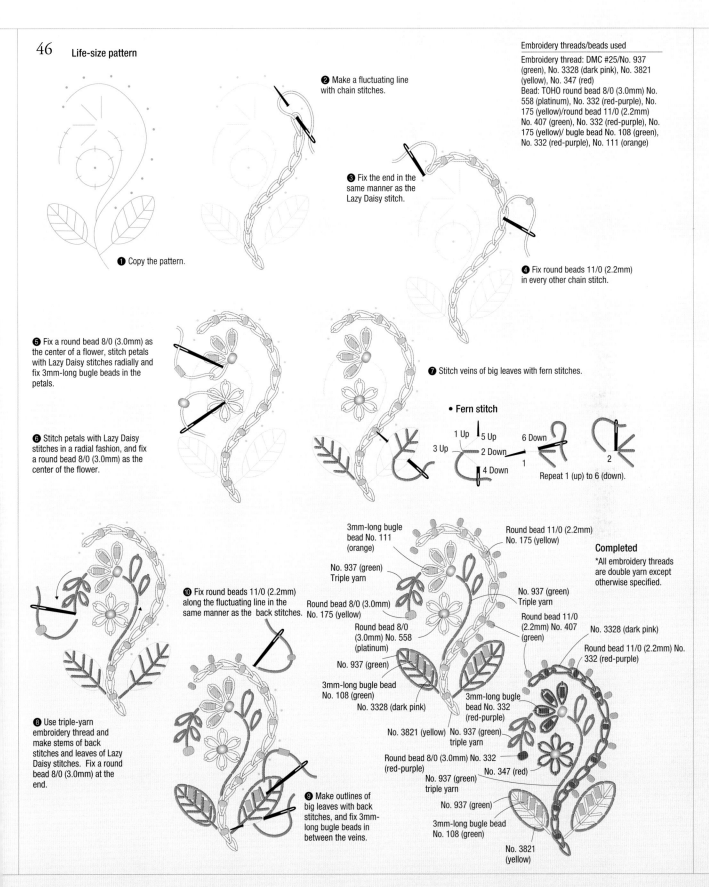

Embroidery threads/beads used

Embroidery thread: DMC #25/No. 937 (green), No. 3328 (dark pink), No. 3821 (yellow), No. 347 (red)
Bead: TOHO round bead 8/0 (3.0mm) No. 558 (platinum), No. 332 (red-purple), No. 175 (yellow)/round bead 11/0 (2.2mm) No. 407 (green), No. 332 (red-purple), No. 175 (yellow)/ bugle bead No. 108 (green), No. 332 (red-purple), No. 111 (orange)

❶ Copy the pattern.

❷ Make a fluctuating line with chain stitches.

❸ Fix the end in the same manner as the Lazy Daisy stitch.

❹ Fix round beads 11/0 (2.2mm) in every other chain stitch.

❺ Fix a round bead 8/0 (3.0mm) as the center of a flower, stitch petals with Lazy Daisy stitches radially and fix 3mm-long bugle beads in the petals.

❻ Stitch petals with Lazy Daisy stitches in a radial fashion, and fix a round bead 8/0 (3.0mm) as the center of the flower.

❼ Stitch veins of big leaves with fern stitches.

• Fern stitch

1 Up   5 Up   6 Down
3 Up   2 Down
       4 Down   1
                    2

Repeat 1 (up) to 6 (down).

❽ Use triple-yarn embroidery thread and make stems of back stitches and leaves of Lazy Daisy stitches. Fix a round bead 8/0 (3.0mm) at the end.

❿ Fix round beads 11/0 (2.2mm) along the fluctuating line in the same manner as the back stitches.

❾ Make outlines of big leaves with back stitches, and fix 3mm-long bugle beads in between the veins.

3mm-long bugle bead No. 111 (orange)

Round bead 11/0 (2.2mm) No. 175 (yellow)

No. 937 (green) Triple yarn

No. 937 (green) Triple yarn

Round bead 8/0 (3.0mm) No. 175 (yellow)

Round bead 8/0 (3.0mm) No. 558 (platinum)

Round bead 11/0 (2.2mm) No. 407 (green)

No. 3328 (dark pink)

Round bead 11/0 (2.2mm) No. 332 (red-purple)

No. 937 (green)

3mm-long bugle bead No. 108 (green)

No. 3328 (dark pink)

3mm-long bugle bead No. 332 (red-purple)

No. 3821 (yellow)   No. 937 (green) triple yarn

Round bead 8/0 (3.0mm) No. 332 (red-purple)

No. 347 (red)

No. 937 (green) triple yarn

No. 937 (green)

3mm-long bugle bead No. 108 (green)

No. 3821 (yellow)

Completed

*All embroidery threads are double yarn except otherwise specified.

47-a

Life-size pattern

*All embroidery threads are
 triple yarn.

Embroidery threads/beads used
_____

Embroidery thread: DMC #25/No. 3862
(brown), No. 772 (light green), No. 3346
(green), BLANC (white)
Bead: TOHO round bead 8/0 (3.0mm),
11/0 (2.2mm) No. 121 (white), No. 902
(yellow)/3mm-long bugle bead No. 121
(white)

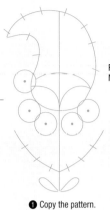

❶ Copy the pattern.

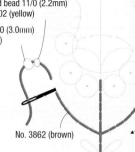

Round bead 11/0 (2.2mm)
No. 902 (yellow)

Round bead 8/0 (3.0mm)
No. 121 (white)

No. 3862 (brown)

• Back stitch

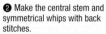

2 Down

Starting
point
1 Up

3 Up

❷ Make the central stem and
symmetrical whips with back
stitches.
*Add beads at the start and end
 points of whips.

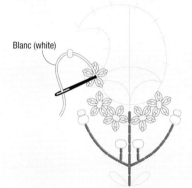

Blanc (white)

❸ Make five petals with Lazy Daisy stitches
in a radial fashion, and fix round beads 11/0
(2.2mm) in the center of the flowers. (Refer
to the page on the right.)

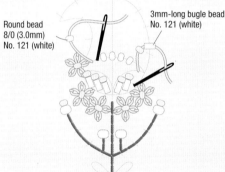

Round bead
8/0 (3.0mm)
No. 121 (white)

3mm-long bugle bead
No. 121 (white)

❹ Fix beads on the central lines in the
same manner as the straight stitch and
back stitch respectively from bottom up.

❺ Make flowers of Lazy Daisy
stitches on the central line.

No. 772 (light green)

No. 3346 (green)

❻ Make leaves of Lazy Daisy stitches along
the stem and whips made in ❷.

❼ Pass light green thread through a needle and green
thread through another, and stitch the fluctuating
line from the lower right toward the upper left (★
). Displace the outer and inner leaves by a few inches
while stitching alternately. Fix round beads 11/0
(2.2mm) in the same manner as the backstitches.

Completed

❽ In the same way, stitch the left line
from the bottom to the upper left (★).

Life-size pattern

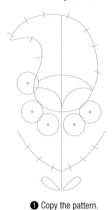

❶ Copy the pattern.

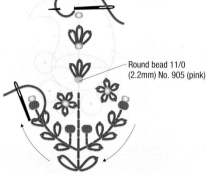

*All embroidery threads are triple yarn.

Round bead 11/0 (2.2mm) No. 558 (platinum)

Round bead 8/0 (3.0mm) No. 405 (red)

Color Variation No. 4205 (reddish)

Starting point

❷ Make the central stem and symmetrical whips with back stitches.
*Add beads at the start and end points of the whips.

Round bead 11/0 (2.2mm) No. 905 (pink)

❸ With thread of the same color, make leaves along the stem and whips with Lazy Daisy stitches, and continuously make flowers in the central part.

Embroidery threads/beads used

Embroidery thread: DMC #25/No. 4205 (reddish), No. 115 (reddish), BLANC (white)
Bead: TOHO round bead 8/0 (3.0mm) No. 405 (red)/round bead 11/0 (2.2mm) No. 405 (red), No. 905 (pink), No. 558 (platinum)/3mm-long bugle bead No. 332 (red-purple)

❹ Change the thread and make bead flowers (refer to the illustration below).

3mm-long bugle bead No. 332 (red-purple)

❺ Fix beads in the central part, for example a set of round beads 11/0 (2.2mm) and 3mm-long bugle bead.

Round bead 11/0 (2.2mm) No. 405 (red)

Completed

❻ Change the thread and make fluctuating lines from the bottom to ★, adding beads.

• Flower of Lazy Daisy stitches

Draw a circle of the same size as the flower you want to make.

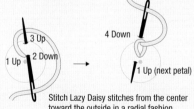

3 Up
1 Up 2 Down
4 Down
1 Up (next petal)

Stitch Lazy Daisy stitches from the center toward the outside in a radial fashion.
*Align the end of the loop on the circle.

Make five stitches evenly and fix a bead in the center.
*Bring the needle up from the back and leave a space for a bead when you bring the needle down to the back, so that the bead is firmly fixed.

Draw a centerline as a guide.

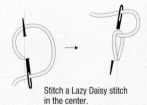

Stitch a Lazy Daisy stitch in the center.

Then stitch Lazy Daisy stitches to the right and left to make a fan shape.

Fix a bead to the root of the stitches.to make a fan shape.

47-c

Life-size pattern

Embroidery threads/beads used

Embroidery thread: DMC #25/No. 3011 (olive), ECRU (natural undyed color)
Bead: TOHO round bead 8/0 (3.0mm), round bead 11/0 (2.2mm), 3mm-long bugle bead No. 332 (red-purple)/round bead 11/0 (2.2mm) No. 901 (yellow), No. 905 (pink), No. 558 (platinum), No. 403 (aqua), No. 122 (milky)/3mm-long bugle bead No. 108 (green)

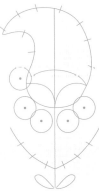

❶ Copy the pattern.

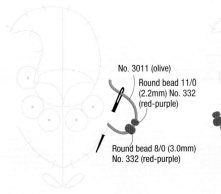

No. 3011 (olive)

Round bead 11/0 (2.2mm) No. 332 (red-purple)

Round bead 8/0 (3.0mm) No. 332 (red-purple)

❷ Make the central stem and symmetrical whips with backstitches. *Add beads at the start and end points of the whips.

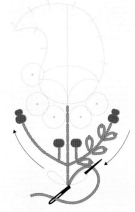

❸ With thread of the same color, make leaves with Lazy Daisy stitches.

• Bead flower

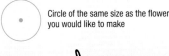

Circle of the same size as the flower you would like to make

3 Up
2 Down
1 Up

Fix a round bead 11/0 (2.2mm) in the center.

Fix six (6) beads in a circular pattern in the same manner as the backstitch.

ECRU (natural undyed color)

Round bead 11/0 (2.2mm) No. 905 (pink)

Round bead 11/0 (2.2mm) No. 901 (yellow)

Round bead 11/0 (2.2mm) No. 558 (platinum)

Round bead 11/0 (2.2mm) No. 122 (milky)

❹ Make flowers of round beads 11/0 (2.2mm).

3mm-long bugle bead No. 332 (red-purple)

Round bead 11/0 (2.2mm) No. 403 (aqua)

3mm-long bugle bead No. 108 (green)

❺ With thread of the same color, fix beads in the central part from the bottom up in the same manner as the straight stitch.

❻ Stitch the fluctuating line from the lower right toward the upper left (★). Displace the outer and inner leaves by a few inches while alternating stitches. Fix round beads 11/0 (2.2mm) in the same manner as the backstitches.

Completed

❼ In the same way, stitch the left line from the bottom to the upper left (★).

48

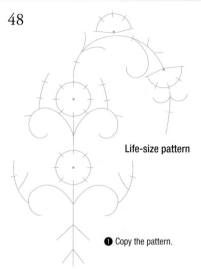

Life-size pattern

❶ Copy the pattern.

Tips for stitching

• Stitch stem (brown) first and then stitch leaves (green/
light green).

• When you stitch leaves, pass green embroidery thread
through a needle and light green embroidery threads
through another.

• Finally, fix beads with white embroidery thread.

Embroidery threads/beads used

Embroidery thread: DMC #25/
No. 3862 (brown), No. 772 (light
green), No. 3346 (green), BLANC
(white) / Bead: TOHO round bead
8/0 (3.0mm), 11/0 (2.2mm), 3mm-
long bugle bead No. 121 (white),
round bead 8/0 (3.0mm) No. 908
(pink), round bead 11/0 (2.2mm)
No. 911 (dark pink)

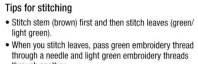

3mm-long bugle bead
No. 121 (white)

No. 3346 (green)

No. 772 (light green)

No. 3862 (brown)

Round bead 11/0 (2.2mm)
No. 121 (white)

Round bead 8/0 (3.0mm)
No. 121 (white)

Round bead 8/0
(3.0mm) No. 908
(pink)

Round bead 11/0 (2.2mm)
No. 911 (dark pink)

Fix all beads with embroidery
thread of BLANC (white).

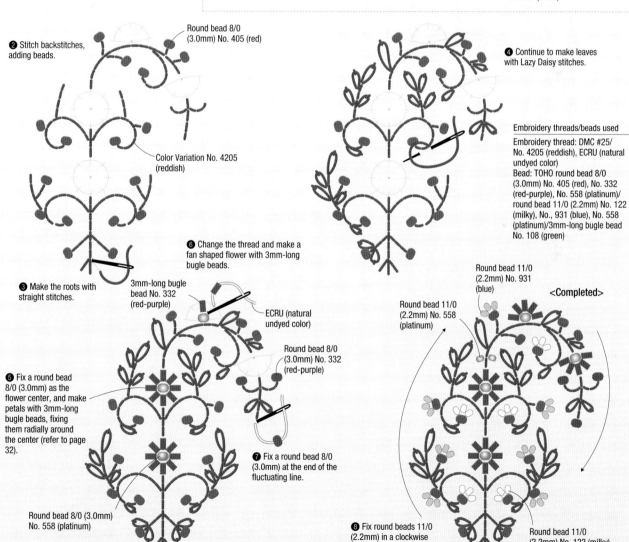

❷ Stitch backstitches,
adding beads.

Round bead 8/0
(3.0mm) No. 405 (red)

Color Variation No. 4205
(reddish)

❸ Make the roots with
straight stitches.

❹ Continue to make leaves
with Lazy Daisy stitches.

Embroidery threads/beads used

Embroidery thread: DMC #25/
No. 4205 (reddish), ECRU (natural
undyed color)
Bead: TOHO round bead 8/0
(3.0mm) No. 405 (red), No. 332
(red-purple), No. 558 (platinum)/
round bead 11/0 (2.2mm) No. 122
(milky), No., 931 (blue), No. 558
(platinum)/3mm-long bugle bead
No. 108 (green)

❻ Change the thread and make a
fan shaped flower with 3mm-long
bugle beads.

3mm-long bugle
bead No. 332
(red-purple)

ECRU (natural
undyed color)

Round bead 8/0
(3.0mm) No. 332
(red-purple)

❺ Fix a round bead
8/0 (3.0mm) as the
flower center, and make
petals with 3mm-long
bugle beads, fixing
them radially around
the center (refer to page
32).

❼ Fix a round bead 8/0
(3.0mm) at the end of the
fluctuating line.

Round bead 8/0 (3.0mm)
No. 558 (platinum)

❽ Fix round beads 11/0
(2.2mm) in a clockwise
fashion.

Round bead 11/0
(2.2mm) No. 931
(blue)

Round bead 11/0
(2.2mm) No. 558
(platinum)

<Completed>

Round bead 11/0
(2.2mm) No. 122 (milky)

49 Stitch colorful flowers of beads on the branches and leaves made with embroidery thread.

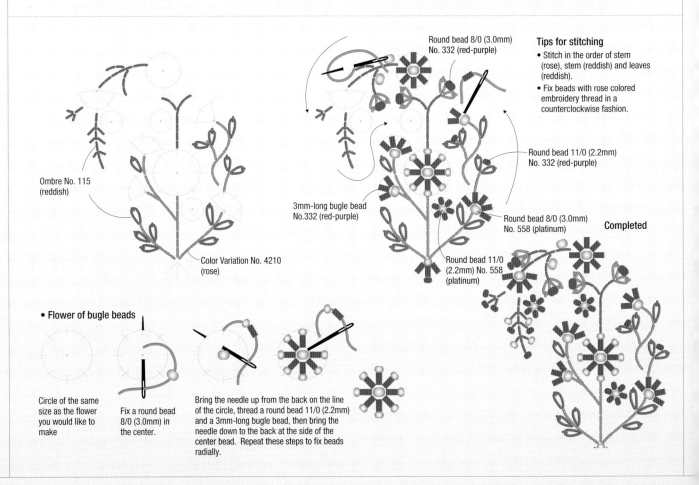

Ombre No. 115
(reddish)

Color Variation No. 4210
(rose)

Round bead 8/0 (3.0mm)
No. 332 (red-purple)

Round bead 11/0 (2.2mm)
No. 332 (red-purple)

3mm-long bugle bead
No.332 (red-purple)

Round bead 8/0 (3.0mm)
No. 558 (platinum)

Round bead 11/0
(2.2mm) No. 558
(platinum)

Tips for stitching
- Stitch in the order of stem (rose), stem (reddish) and leaves (reddish).
- Fix beads with rose colored embroidery thread in a counterclockwise fashion.

Completed

• Flower of bugle beads

Circle of the same size as the flower you would like to make

Fix a round bead 8/0 (3.0mm) in the center.

Bring the needle up from the back on the line of the circle, thread a round bead 11/0 (2.2mm) and a 3mm-long bugle bead, then bring the needle down to the back at the side of the center bead. Repeat these steps to fix beads radially.

49. Paisley on the left page

Embroidery threads/beads used

Embroidery thread: DMC #25/No. 3862 (brown), No. 772 (light green), BLANC (white) / Bead: TOHO round bead 8/0 (3.0mm), 11/0 (2.2mm) No. 332 (red-purple), No. 901 (yellow), No. 905 (pink), No. 558 (platinum) / 3mm-long bugle bead No. 121 (white), No. 332 (red-purple), No. 108 (green)

49. Paisley on the right page

Embroidery threads/beads used

Embroidery thread: DMC #25/No. 4210 (rose), No. 115 (reddish) / Bead: TOHO round bead 8/0 (3.0mm), 11/0 (2.2mm) No. 332 (red-purple), No. 558 (platinum) / 3mm-long bugle bead No. 332 (red-purple)

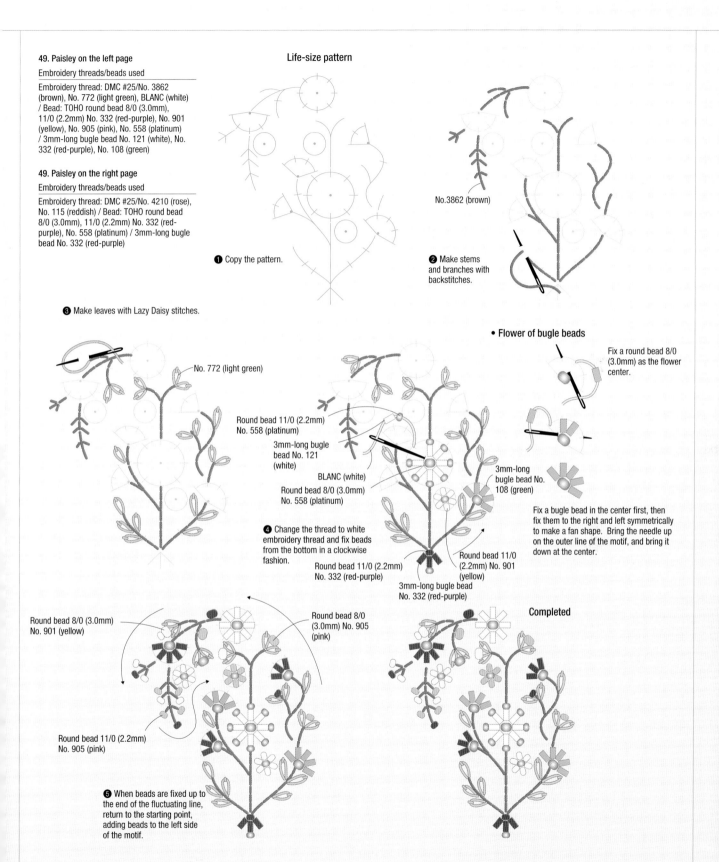

Life-size pattern

❶ Copy the pattern.

No.3862 (brown)

❷ Make stems and branches with backstitches.

❸ Make leaves with Lazy Daisy stitches.

No. 772 (light green)

Round bead 11/0 (2.2mm) No. 558 (platinum)

3mm-long bugle bead No. 121 (white)

BLANC (white)

Round bead 8/0 (3.0mm) No. 558 (platinum)

❹ Change the thread to white embroidery thread and fix beads from the bottom in a clockwise fashion.

Round bead 11/0 (2.2mm) No. 332 (red-purple)

3mm-long bugle bead No. 332 (red-purple)

Round bead 11/0 (2.2mm) No. 901 (yellow)

3mm-long bugle bead No. 108 (green)

• Flower of bugle beads

Fix a round bead 8/0 (3.0mm) as the flower center.

Fix a bugle bead in the center first, then fix them to the right and left symmetrically to make a fan shape. Bring the needle up on the outer line of the motif, and bring it down at the center.

Round bead 8/0 (3.0mm) No. 901 (yellow)

Round bead 8/0 (3.0mm) No. 905 (pink)

Round bead 11/0 (2.2mm) No. 905 (pink)

❺ When beads are fixed up to the end of the fluctuating line, return to the starting point, adding beads to the left side of the motif.

Completed

CREWEL
Scandinavian Motif 1
with Beads

stitch design
50

stitch design
51

stitch design
52

Basics of Crewel Work

Let's try this technique on a Scandinavian motif represented with loosely twisted wool yarn. Happily stitch away if you're in the mood to color a picture, using Appleton's crewel wool which is abundantly available in a number of colors!

Let's try Scandinavian motif 51!

Crewel Work

Crewel means loosely twisted, worsted embroidery thread available in many colors. It seems that the word comes from "clue (yarn ball)" in Anglo-Saxon. Crewel work has existed since the 16th century, which refers to embroidery using crewel thread. Crewel work features muted colors of natural dye and dynamic, simplified and naturalistic design. American Crewel work, started by immigrants to America, introduced several familiar plant and animal designs. In addition, since it was difficult to procure the materials, the Romanian stitch was often used to minimize the amount of wool yarn on the back of the fabric.

① Put the fabric, one-sided paper chalk, pattern copied on tracing paper or something similar and finally cellophane, in that order, then trace the pattern with tracer (metallic pencil).

② When you find it difficult to draw the pattern with paper chalk on fluffy wool fabric or loose fabric, redraw the pattern with pencil-type chalk.

Life-size pattern

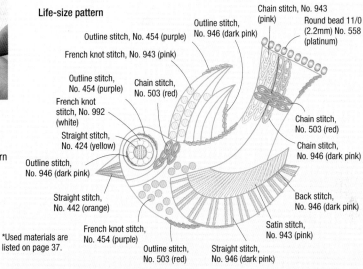

Chain stitch, No. 943 (pink)
Round bead 11/0 (2.2mm) No. 558 (platinum)
Outline stitch, No. 946 (dark pink)
Outline stitch, No. 454 (purple)
French knot stitch, No. 943 (pink)
Chain stitch, No. 503 (red)
Outline stitch, No. 454 (purple)
French knot stitch, No. 992 (white)
Chain stitch, No. 503 (red)
Straight stitch, No. 424 (yellow)
Chain stitch, No. 946 (dark pink)
Outline stitch, No. 946 (dark pink)
Straight stitch, No. 442 (orange)
Back stitch, No. 946 (dark pink)
French knot stitch, No. 454 (purple)
Satin stitch, No. 943 (pink)
*Used materials are listed on page 37.
Outline stitch, No. 503 (red)
Straight stitch, No. 946 (dark pink)

Tip When you have difficulty passing wool yarn through a needle, fold the edge of a sewing thread and pass it through the needle, then pass the wool yarn through the loop of sewing thread and pull out the sewing thread.

Start

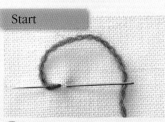   

③ Bring the needle up from the back, and stitch the thread coming out of the fabric. With this method, the thread is fixed without making a knot.

④ First, fill the back and tail parts with chain stitches.

⑤ Then stitch the neck and the base of the tail with chain stitches, and the upper part of the wing with satin stitches, the lower part with straight stitches.

⑥ Stitch the center of the eye with satin stitches, and surround it with French knot stitches. In addition, rim the eye with outline stitches.

⑦ Make the outline with outline stitches, stitch the wing in the back, and fill the chest part with French knot stitches.

⑧ Make the beak with straight stitches.

Complete!

⑨ Finally, fix beads to the tip of tail. When you want to use round bead 8/0 (3.0mm), fix beads while stitching the outline with backstitches.

CREWEL

❶ Copy the pattern (on page 75) to the desired size and copy it onto the fabric.

❷ Make the thick stem in the center with chain stitches, and stitch outline stitches on both sides of the stem.

❸ Make the stem extend transversely with outline stitches. and stitch outline stitches on both sides of the stem.

❹ Make half of the leaves with satin stitches and the other part with straight stitches using green thread. Lastly, stitch around the straight stitches and the veins with outline stitches.

❺ Stitch small branches and leaves, berries and buds.

❻ Fill the inside of the flowers on the right and left with satin stitches and long and short stitches.

❼ Edge the flower outline and switching part with outline stitches.

❽ Make the central flower. Start with satin stitches in the center and surround it with yellow petals, and make circles toward the outside in a concentric fashion.

❾ For the outer petals, make the inside with satin stitches using pink thread, and surround it with satin stitches using dark pink thread. Edge the petals with double lines of chain stitches.

❿ Make stamens and pistils between the petals with outline stitches and satin stitches.

⓫ Stitch birds facing each other in the upper part, and adorn the surrounding area with French knot stitches and double cross stitches.

Tip   Commonly used basic stitches

Outline stitch

Stitch from left to right, returning halfway. You can make a clean curved line with this stitch, and you can also adjust the thickness.

Chain stitch

This stitch is made by linking small loops like a chain. You can make a specific curve line with this stitch. It is also used to fill the surface.

French knot stitch

This stitch is made by wrapping the thread coming out of the fabric around the needle to make a knot. You can enjoy a three-dimensional texture if you use this to fill in a certain part.

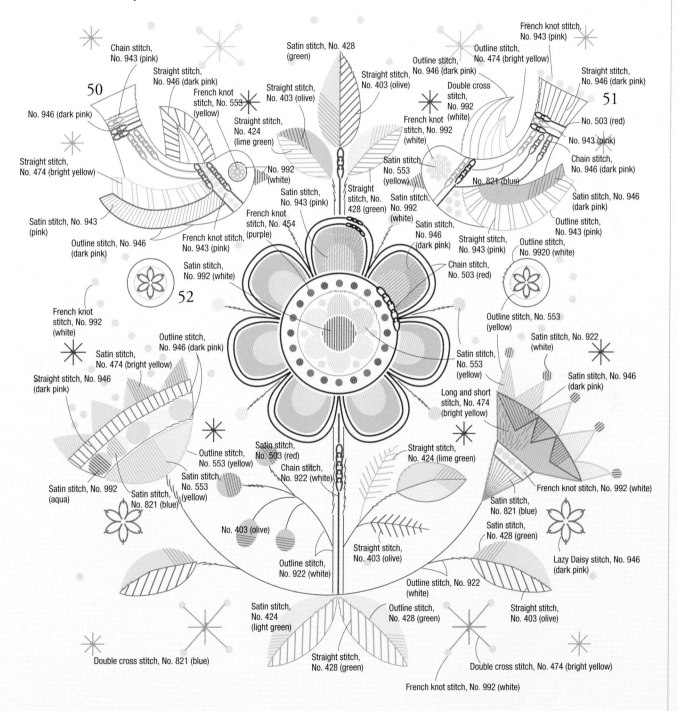

Embroidery threads/beads used

Appleton Crewel wool No. 821 (blue), No. 943 (pink), No.946 (dark pink), No. 503 (red), No. 553 (yellow), No. 474 (bright yellow), No. 424 (lime green), No. 428 (green), No. 403 (olive), No. 992 (white)

Stitches and embroidery threads used

CREWEL
Floral Motif
with Beads

stitch design
53

stitch design
54

stitch design
55

stitch design
56

stitch design
57

stitch design
58

stitch design
59

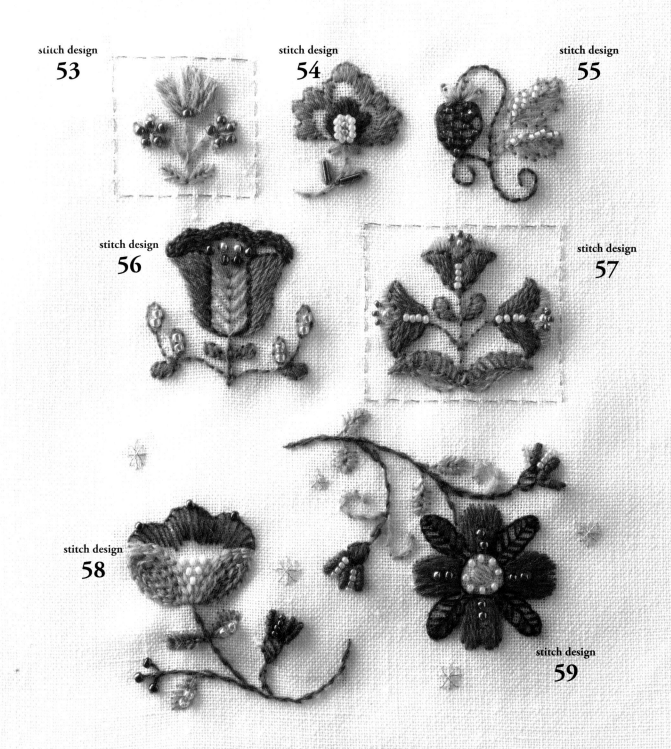

Adding beads to Crewel Work...

55 Make a strawberry with trellis stitches. Add beads to the cross points to make a pebbly texture.

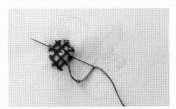

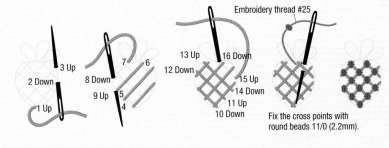

Embroidery thread #25

3 Up
2 Down
1 Up

7   6
8 Down
9 Up   5   4

13 Up   16 Down
12 Down
15 Up
14 Down
11 Up
10 Down

Fix the cross points with round beads 11/0 (2.2mm).

❶ Make a strawberry with trellis stitches. Stitch at an angle in a reticular pattern, and fix the cross points with round beads 11/0 (2.2mm).

❷ Make the strawberry outline with backstitches.

❸ Make stems with backstitches. Start from the edge of the strawberry.

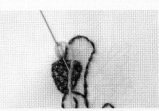

❹ Make a strawberry calyx with double Lazy Daisy stitches. Make Lazy Daisy stitches according to the pattern, and then make smaller Lazy Daisy stitches inside those.

❺ Make half of the inside of a leaf with straight stitches.

❻ Make the outline of the leaf with backstitches.

❼ Continuously make the center vein and the stem with backstitches.

❽ Change the thread to embroidery thread #25, and add round beads 11/0 (2.2mm) to the remaining half of the inside of the leaf, in the same manner as the straight stitches.

Completed

Embroidery threads/beads used

Embroidery thread: Appleton Crewel wool No. 758 (red), No. 947 (pink), No. 544 (lime green), No. 245 (dark green)/DMC #25/No. 347 (red), No. 937 (green) / Bead: Round bead 11/0 (2.2mm) No. 241 (red), No. 945 (lime green)

Stitches

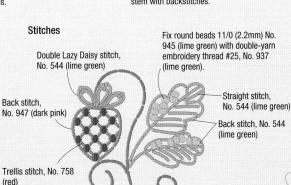

Double Lazy Daisy stitch, No. 544 (lime green)

Fix round beads 11/0 (2.2mm) No. 945 (lime green) with double-yarn embroidery thread #25, No. 937 (lime green).

Back stitch, No. 947 (dark pink)

Straight stitch, No. 544 (lime green)

Back stitch, No. 544 (lime green)

Trellis stitch, No. 758 (red)
Fix round beads 11/0 (2.2mm) No. 241 (red) with double-yarn embroidery thread #25, No. 347 (red).

Back stitch, No. 245 (dark green)

Life-size pattern

CREWEL

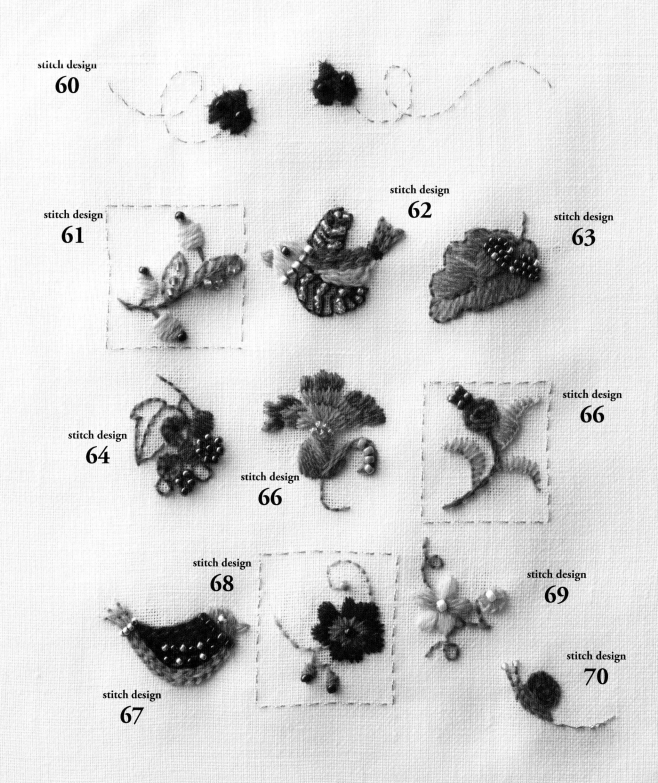

stitch design
60

stitch design
61

stitch design
62

stitch design
63

stitch design
64

stitch design
66

stitch design
66

stitch design
68

stitch design
67

stitch design
69

stitch design
70

Adding beads to Crewel Work...

62 Fill the torso with chain stitches and outline stitches to make a three-dimensional motif.

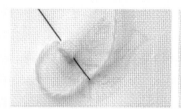

❶ Fill the head part with satin stitches. Start from the center and fill the upper half first, then return to the center and fill the lower half.

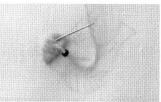

❷ Fix a round bead 8/0 (3.0mm) as an eye. Insert a needle into a point allowing 1 round bead 8/0 (3.0mm) from the point where the needle comes out.

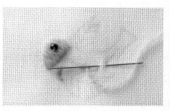

❸ Fill the belly with outline stitches.

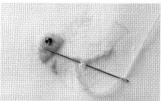

❹ Stitch the 2nd row and subsequent rows tightly, in the same direction as the 1st row (from left to right).

❺ Change the thread and fill the back with chain stitches.

❻ Stitch the 2nd and 3rd rows tightly, in the same direction as the 1st row (from left to right).

❼ Change the thread and make the left wing with straight stitches in an arrow feather pattern. The direction of the arrow feather creates a suggestion of a wing.

❽ Edge the wing with backstitches.

❾ Add round beads 8/0 (3.0mm) to the neck in the same manner as the backstitch.

❿ Make satin stitches in the manner of collecting up the base of the tail.

⓫ Add round beads 11/0 (2.2mm) with embroidery thread #25 in between the stitches making up the wing, in the same manner as stitching the arrow feather pattern.

⓬ Change the thread and make the beak with straight stitches to complete.

Complete

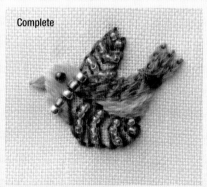

Embroidery threads/beads used
Embroidery thread: Appleton Crewel wool No. 565 (blue), No. 561 (aqua), No. 454 (purple), No. 473 (bright yellow)
Bead: Round bead 8/0 (3.0mm), No. 332 (red-purple), No. 264 (turquoise), No. 558 (platinum)/round bead 11/0 (2.2mm), No. 163 (blue)

Stitches

Fix a round bead 8/0 (3.0mm) No. 332 (red-purple) with embroidery thread No. 561 (aqua).

Add round beads 11/0 (2.2mm), No. 163 (blue) with double-yarn embroidery thread #25, No. 827 (aqua).

Straight stitch, No. 473 (bright yellow)

Fill with chain stitches, No. 565 (blue).

Satin stitch, No. 561 (aqua)

Satin stitch, No. 454 (purple)

Fill with outline stitches, No. 561 (aqua).

Back stitch, No. 454 (purple)

Fix round beads 8/0 (3.0mm) No. 558 (platinum) and No. 264 (turquoise) alternately with embroidery thread No. 454 (purple).

Straight stitch, No. 454 (purple)

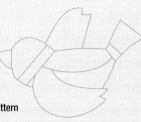

Life-size pattern

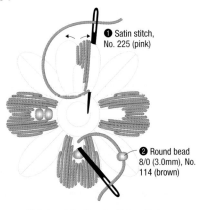

❶ Satin stitch, No. 225 (pink)

❷ Round bead 8/0 (3.0mm), No. 114 (brown)

❶ Make petals with satin stitches. Start from the recessed part in the center, stitch the half part and then stitch the other side symmetrically.

❷ Add round beads 8/0 (3.0mm) one by one in the center of the petals in the same manner as the backstitch.

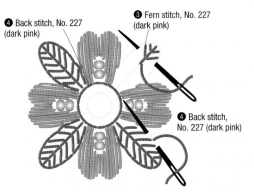

❹ Back stitch, No. 227 (dark pink)

❸ Fern stitch, No. 227 (dark pink)

❹ Back stitch, No. 227 (dark pink)

❸ Make the inside of another type of petals with fern stitches.

❹ Make outlines of petals and the flower center with backstitches.

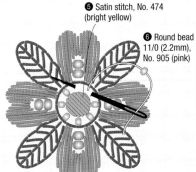

❺ Satin stitch, No. 474 (bright yellow)

❻ Round bead 11/0 (2.2mm), No. 905 (pink)

❺ Fill the central part of the flower center with satin stitches.

❻ Add round beads 11/0 (2.2mm) with embroidery thread #25, No. 761 (pale pink) around the center made of satin stitches, in the same manner as the backstitches.

*Appleton Crewel Wool (wool yarn) is used unless otherwise specified.

❼ Make petals of small flowers with bullion stitches and round beads 11/0 (2.2mm).

*Stitch with double-yarn Crewel Wool.

• Bullion stitch

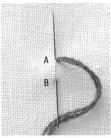

A
B

❶ Pass the needle in and out of the fabric, taking care not to stitch the thread. (The length from A to B is the length of the stitch.)

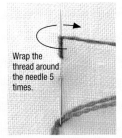

Wrap the thread around the needle 5 times.

❷ Wrap the thread around the needle, pressing the thread down each time to close. Take care not to overlap the thread.

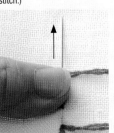

❸ Steady the wrapped part with a thumb and pull the needle out, taking care not to loosen the thread.

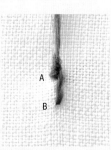

A
B

❹ Draw the thread up tightly enough to wrinkle the fabric.

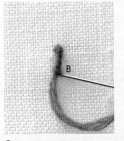

A
B

❺ Bring down the thread and align it with the end of wrapping B. Adjust the wrapped part with the tip of the needle.

B

❻ Insert the needle into B

❼ The bullion stitch is completed.

Embroidery threads/beads used

Embroidery thread: Appleton Crewel wool
No. 225 (pink), No. 227 (dark pink), No. 245
(dark green), No. 544 (lime green), No. 474
(bright yellow)/DMC #25/No. 761 (pink)/
Bead: Round bead 8/0 (3.0mm), No. 114
(brown)/round bead 11/0 (2.2mm), No. 905
(pink)

Life-size pattern

❽ Make the inside of a calyx of small flowers
with straight stitches, and make the outline
with backstitches.

❾ Make stems of dark green with outline
stitches. Start from the base of the flower or
calyx.

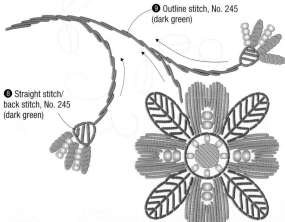

❾ Outline stitch, No. 245
(dark green)

❽ Straight stitch/
back stitch, No. 245
(dark green)

• Outline stitch

❿ Leaf stitch/back stitch, No. 544 (lime green)

⓫ Outline stitch, No. 544 (lime green)

• Leaf stitch

Stitch from the
inside towards the
outside.

Make the
center vein with
backstitches.

❿ Make leaves with leaf stitches,
and continue to make the veins and
stems with backstitches.

⓫ Make thin stems with outline
stitches.

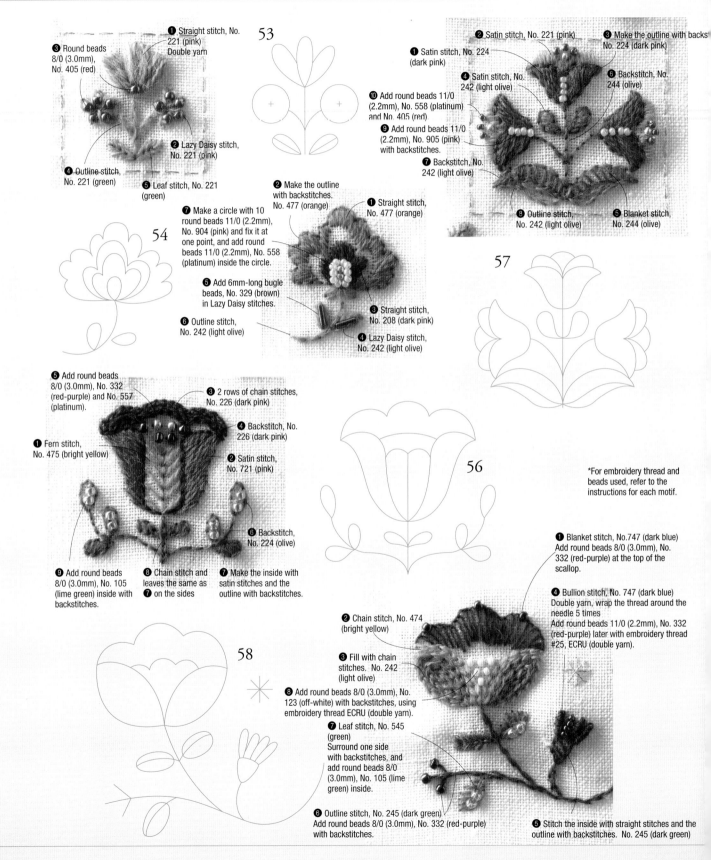

53

❶ Straight stitch, No. 221 (pink) Double yarn

❸ Round beads 8/0 (3.0mm), No. 405 (red)

❷ Lazy Daisy stitch, No. 221 (pink)

❹ Outline stitch, No. 221 (green)

❺ Leaf stitch, No. 221 (green)

❷ Satin stitch, No. 221 (pink)

❶ Satin stitch, No. 224 (dark pink)

❸ Make the outline with backs. No. 224 (dark pink)

❹ Satin stitch, No. 242 (light olive)

❻ Backstitch, No. 244 (olive)

❿ Add round beads 11/0 (2.2mm), No. 558 (platinum) and No. 405 (red)

❾ Add round beads 11/0 (2.2mm), No. 905 (pink) with backstitches.

❼ Backstitch, No. 242 (light olive)

❽ Outline stitch, No. 242 (light olive)

❺ Blanket stitch, No. 244 (olive)

54

❼ Make a circle with 10 round beads 11/0 (2.2mm), No. 904 (pink) and fix it at one point, and add round beads 11/0 (2.2mm), No. 558 (platinum) inside the circle.

❷ Make the outline with backstitches. No. 477 (orange)

❶ Straight stitch, No. 477 (orange)

❺ Add 6mm-long bugle beads, No. 329 (brown) in Lazy Daisy stitches.

❻ Outline stitch, No. 242 (light olive)

❸ Straight stitch, No. 208 (dark pink)

❹ Lazy Daisy stitch, No. 242 (light olive)

57

❺ Add round beads 8/0 (3.0mm), No. 332 (red-purple) and No. 557 (platinum).

❸ 2 rows of chain stitches, No. 226 (dark pink)

❹ Backstitch, No. 226 (dark pink)

❶ Fern stitch, No. 475 (bright yellow)

❷ Satin stitch, No. 721 (pink)

❻ Backstitch, No. 224 (olive)

❾ Add round beads 8/0 (3.0mm), No. 105 (lime green) inside with backstitches.

❽ Chain stitch and leaves the same as ❼ on the sides

❼ Make the inside with satin stitches and the outline with backstitches.

56

*For embroidery thread and beads used, refer to the instructions for each motif.

❶ Blanket stitch, No.747 (dark blue) Add round beads 8/0 (3.0mm), No. 332 (red-purple) at the top of the scallop.

❹ Bullion stitch, No. 747 (dark blue) Double yarn, wrap the thread around the needle 5 times Add round beads 11/0 (2.2mm), No. 332 (red-purple) later with embroidery thread #25, ECRU (double yarn).

58

❷ Chain stitch, No. 474 (bright yellow)

❸ Fill with chain stitches. No. 242 (light olive)

❽ Add round beads 8/0 (3.0mm), No. 123 (off-white) with backstitches, using embroidery thread ECRU (double yarn).

❼ Leaf stitch, No. 545 (green) Surround one side with backstitches, and add round beads 8/0 (3.0mm), No. 105 (lime green) inside.

❻ Outline stitch, No. 245 (dark green) Add round beads 8/0 (3.0mm), No. 332 (red-purple) with backstitches.

❺ Stitch the inside with straight stitches and the outline with backstitches. No. 245 (dark green)

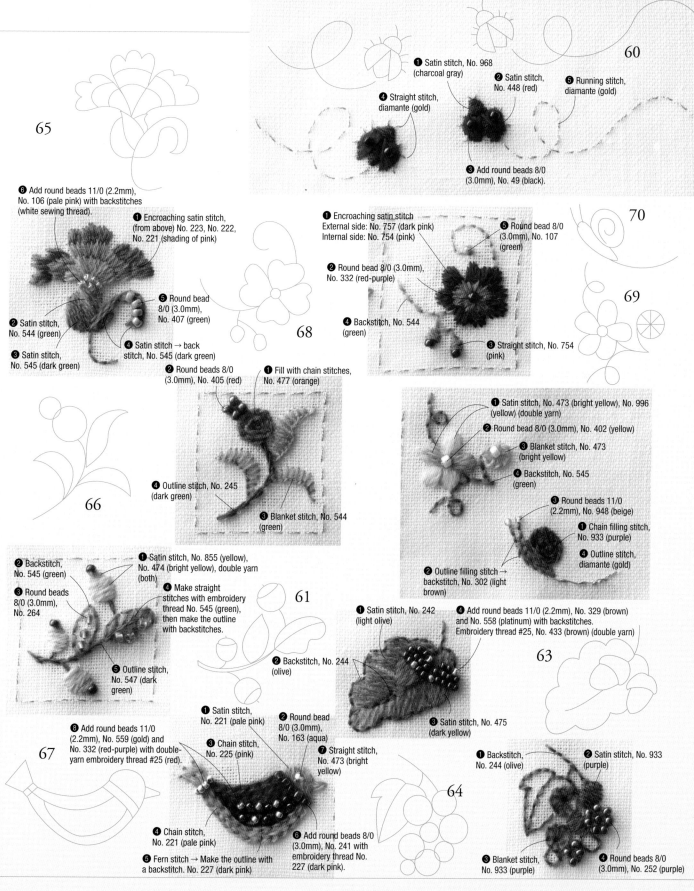

65

60

❶ Satin stitch, No. 968 (charcoal gray)

❷ Satin stitch, No. 448 (red)

❺ Running stitch, diamante (gold)

❹ Straight stitch, diamante (gold)

❸ Add round beads 8/0 (3.0mm), No. 49 (black).

❻ Add round beads 11/0 (2.2mm), No. 106 (pale pink) with backstitches (white sewing thread).

❶ Encroaching satin stitch, (from above) No. 223, No. 222, No. 221 (shading of pink)

❶ Encroaching satin stitch External side: No. 757 (dark pink) Internal side: No. 754 (pink)

❺ Round bead 8/0 (3.0mm), No. 107 (green)

70

❷ Round bead 8/0 (3.0mm), No. 332 (red-purple)

❷ Satin stitch, No. 544 (green)

❺ Round bead 8/0 (3.0mm), No. 407 (green)

68

❹ Backstitch, No. 544 (green)

❸ Straight stitch, No. 754 (pink)

69

❸ Satin stitch, No. 545 (dark green)

❹ Satin stitch → back stitch, No. 545 (dark green)

❷ Round beads 8/0 (3.0mm), No. 405 (red)

❶ Fill with chain stitches, No. 477 (orange)

❶ Satin stitch, No. 473 (bright yellow), No. 996 (yellow) (double yarn)

❷ Round bead 8/0 (3.0mm), No. 402 (yellow)

❸ Blanket stitch, No. 473 (bright yellow)

❹ Backstitch, No. 545 (green)

❹ Outline stitch, No. 245 (dark green)

66

❸ Blanket stitch, No. 544 (green)

❸ Round beads 11/0 (2.2mm), No. 948 (beige)

❶ Chain filling stitch, No. 933 (purple)

❹ Outline stitch, diamante (gold)

❷ Backstitch, No. 545 (green)

❶ Satin stitch, No. 855 (yellow), No. 474 (bright yellow), double yarn (both)

❸ Round beads 8/0 (3.0mm), No. 264

❹ Make straight stitches with embroidery thread No. 545 (green), then make the outline with backstitches.

61

❷ Outline filling stitch → backstitch, No. 302 (light brown)

❶ Satin stitch, No. 242 (light olive)

❹ Add round beads 11/0 (2.2mm), No. 329 (brown) and No. 558 (platinum) with backstitches. Embroidery thread #25, No. 433 (brown) (double yarn)

63

❷ Backstitch, No. 244 (olive)

❺ Outline stitch, No. 547 (dark green)

❽ Add round beads 11/0 (2.2mm), No. 559 (gold) and No. 332 (red-purple) with double-yarn embroidery thread #25 (red).

67

❶ Satin stitch, No. 221 (pale pink)

❷ Round bead 8/0 (3.0mm), No. 163 (aqua)

❸ Chain stitch, No. 225 (pink)

❼ Straight stitch, No. 473 (bright yellow)

❸ Satin stitch, No. 475 (dark yellow)

❶ Backstitch, No. 244 (olive)

❷ Satin stitch, No. 933 (purple)

64

❹ Chain stitch, No. 221 (pale pink)

❺ Fern stitch → Make the outline with a backstitch. No. 227 (dark pink)

❻ Add round beads 8/0 (3.0mm), No. 241 with embroidery thread No. 227 (dark pink).

❸ Blanket stitch, No. 933 (purple)

❹ Round beads 8/0 (3.0mm), No. 252 (purple)

stitch design
71

stitch design
72

stitch design
73

stitch design
74

stitch design
75

stitch design
76

stitch design
77

stitch design
78

Adding beads to surface darning stitches...

71 Carry the thread from edge to edge vertically and horizontally with the same spacing, and pass the horizontal thread in a weaving manner.

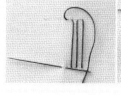

72 Enjoy expressing yourself in a different way by changing the spacing of the horizontal thread.

Surface Darning Stitch

This is called the surface stitch which is used to pierce the outline and carry long threads from edge to edge. Typically it is made by first making stitches vertically, then passing the thread through vertical stitches horizontally.

73 Close up the space vertically and horizontally. Change the shape to look like a heart-shaped cookie.

 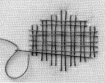 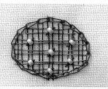

74 Enclose the weave with chain stitches to make a pie motif.

75 Stitch in a square shape at regular intervals, closing up the space.

76 Make a diamond shape with surface stitches.

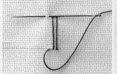  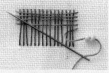 

77 Make plaited stitches by passing the horizontal thread alternately under and over three vertical threads.

 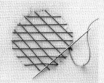

78 Make honeycomb filling stitches. Add beads to make it look like a Belgian waffle.

BASIC LESSON

Couched Trellis Stitches

with Beads

stitch design
79

stitch design
80

stitch design
81

stitch design
82

stitch design
83

Adding beads to Crewel Work...

79   Stitch a grid evenly as a base and fix points of the intersection with half stitches. Add beads, alternating them.

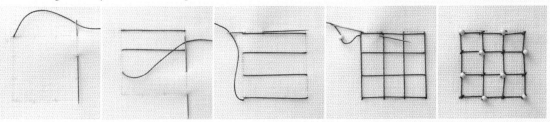

80   Stitch upright cross stitches, alternating them, then add stitches to the base.

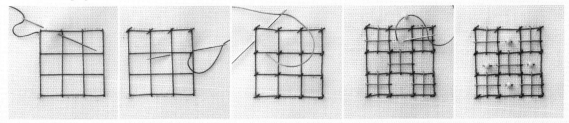

81   Stitch Lazy Daisy stitches radially and add beads in the center to make a flower motif.

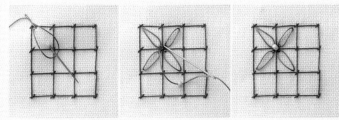

Couched Trellis Stitch

Stitch long stitches in a grid and then fix the points where two threads cross. With different ways of fixing and stitching, you can express yourself in a variety of ways.

82   Lay threads diagonally and fix the intersection points, adding beads.

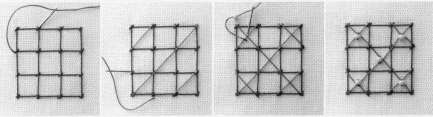

83   Lay threads diagonally to create something different.

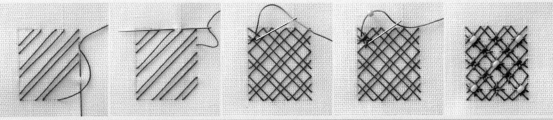

BASIC LESSON

stitch design
84

stitch design
85

stitch design
86

stitch design
87

stitch design
88

stitch design
89

stitch design
90

Adding beads to knotted stitches...

84 To make a checkered chain band, make chains passing threads alternately through the base stitches, splitting the beads.

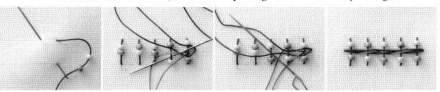

85 Pass the thread across and make knots at the right end, left end and the center in that order. Add beads to make colorful diamond stitches.

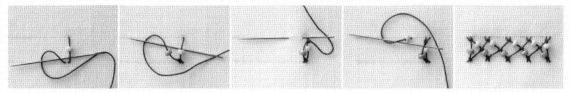

86 Pass the thread through the stitches twice to make knots. Add beads, alternating them. This is a double knot stitch.

Knotted Stitch

This is a generic term for stitches with various knots on the surface of the fabric. Beads are added in knots or stitches here.

87 Wrap the thread twice around the needle before starting the next stitch. This is a Portuguese knotted stem stitch.

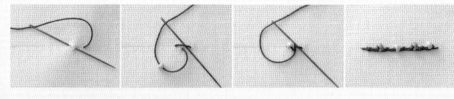

88 This is a variation of the buttonhole stitch. You can use it for edging.

89 Make zigzag stitches and lace another thread through the stitches, adding beads.

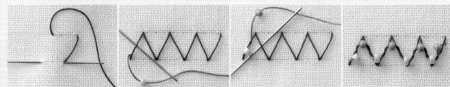

90 Lace a thread through breton stitches made with twisted herringbone stitches.

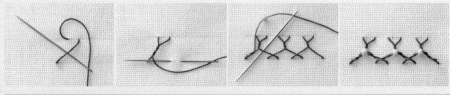

Knotted Stitches with Beads (84-90)

Darning Stitches
with Beads

stitch design
91

stitch design
92

stitch design
93

stitch design
94

stitch design
95

stitch design
96

Adding beads to darning stitches...

> ### Darning Stitch
> Darning means making running stitches along the weaving yarn of the fabric. It is a surface filling technique and was originally used in sewing.

91 Stitch with even spaces. Change the thread color to make a ribbon-like motif.

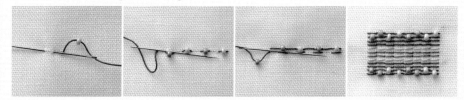

92 Make buttonhole stitches, lining up two stitches, and add beads in between stitches from the 2nd row.

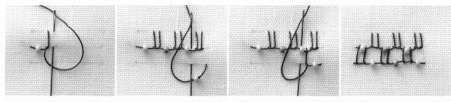

93 Though it looks complicated with making two journeys to and fro, it is a repetition of the same stitch and easy to do. This is called a triangular Turkish stitch.

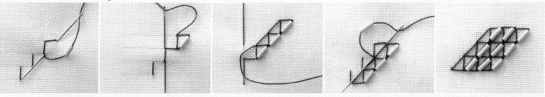

94 Make vertical stitches and return stitching with bugle beads. This is he Bosnian stitch.

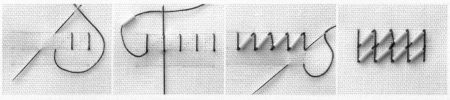

95 Fix bugle beads with running stitches and connect two rows with another thread. This is called the Japanese darning stitch.

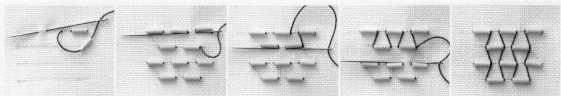

96 Make a sorbello stitch, passing the needle under the thread bar. It looks like a piece of lace when stitched in a row.

Line Stitches

with Beads

stitch design
97

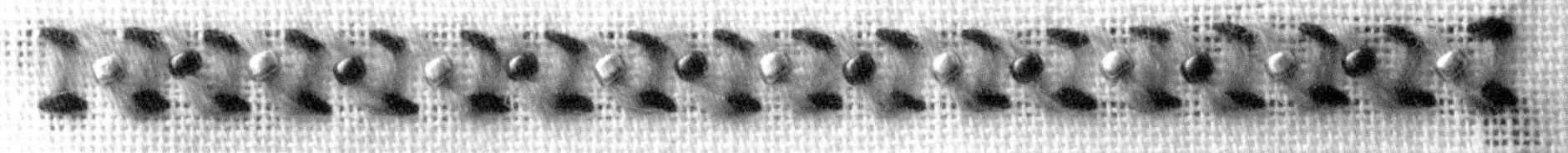

stitch design
98

stitch design
99

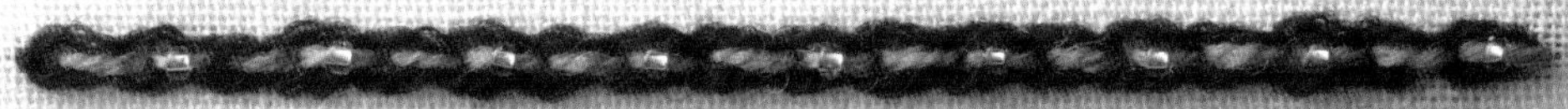

stitch design
100

stitch design
101

stitch design
102

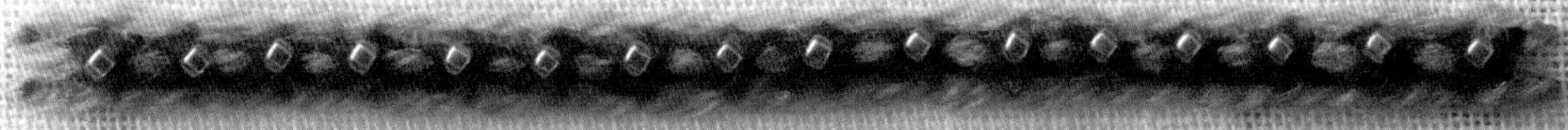

stitch design
103

Adding beads to line stitches...

97 Loop beaded thread around line stitches. You can express yourself in different ways with various color combinations.

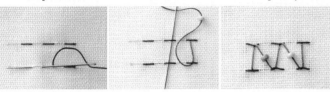

Line Stitch

Stitches which form lines are basic and serve various uses, and are often used to make curved or straight lines. Here are some variations of line stitches.

98 Loop beaded thread loosely around each stitch of the outline stitches.

99 Make chain stitches first, and then make backstitches on top of them with different thread.

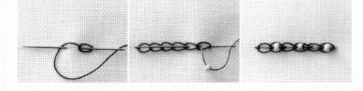

100 This is a variation of chain stitches. Stitch crossways, adding beads.

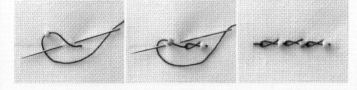

101 Loop beaded thread around chain stitches to make loop-like stitches.

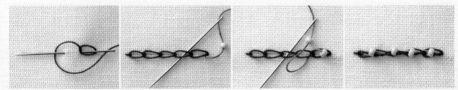

102 Loop beaded thread around uniformed rows of chain stitches alternately to make braid-like stitches.

103 Be careful not to pull the thread too tightly in order to create a soft texture.

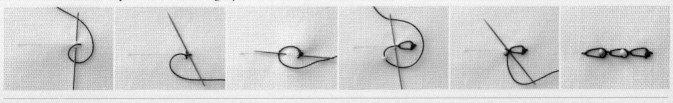

Line Stitches with Beads (97-103)

BASIC LESSON

Filling Stitches Variation

with Beads

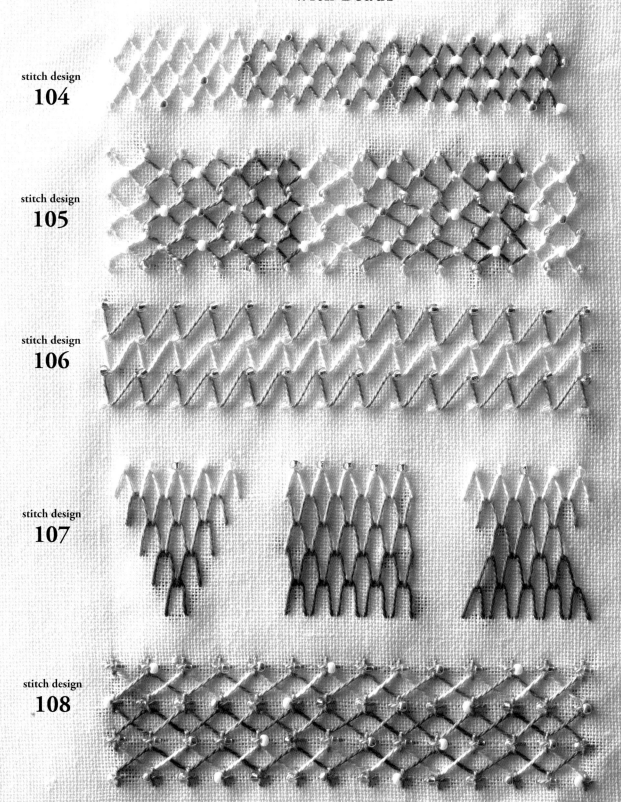

stitch design
104

stitch design
105

stitch design
106

stitch design
107

stitch design
108

Adding beads to variations of filling stitches...

104 To make cloud filling stitches, make vertical stitches as a base and pass other thread through them from left to right.

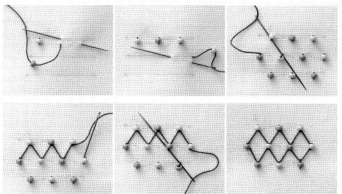

> ### Filling Stitch
>
> Filling means to fill up the surface of the fabric. Here are techniques to lay short stitches first and to pass threads over them, for example the cloud filling stitch.

105 Make base stitches and pass other thread through them up and down. This is called a fancy stitch.

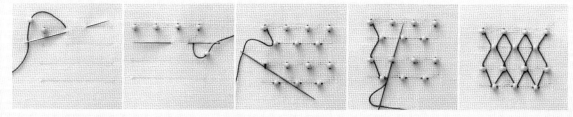

106 Change the thread by row to make a stripe pattern.

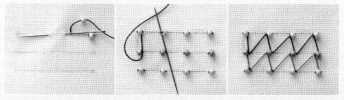

107 You can make various patterns depending on how you pass the thread through the base. This is called an open wave stitch.

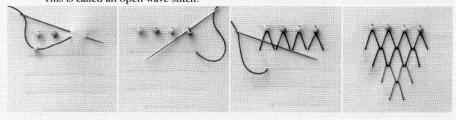

108 Change the thread by row to make a complicated stripe pattern.

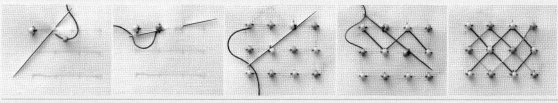

BASIC LESSON

stitch design
109

stitch design
110

stitch design
111

stitch design
112

Adding beads to interlaced cross stitches...

Interlaced Cross Stitch

To interlace means to loop around or cross threads. Using a lattice pattern or herring bone stitches for the base will make this stitch more decorative.

109   Stitch the base squarely, adding beads. This is an interlaced cross stitch.

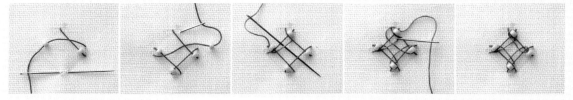

110   Make the base with crossing stitches first, and pass other thread through the base stitches to use it by itself or to make combination patterns.

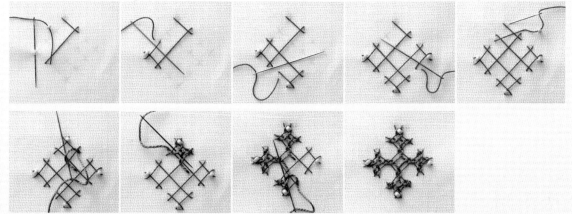

111   This is an application of number 110. Lengthen the base stitches to make a cross motif, like an accessory.

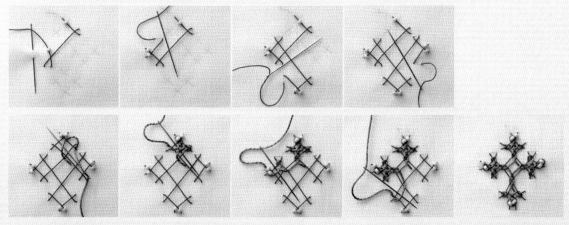

112   This stitch is traditionally used. Loop beaded thread around the double herringbone stitches to make a decorative motif.

Eastern European Motif
with Beads

stitch design
113

stitch design
114

stitch design
115

stitch design
116

stitch design
117

stitch design
118

stitch design
119

stitch design
121

stitch design
120

stitch design
122

Cross stitch charts of Eastern Europe motifs

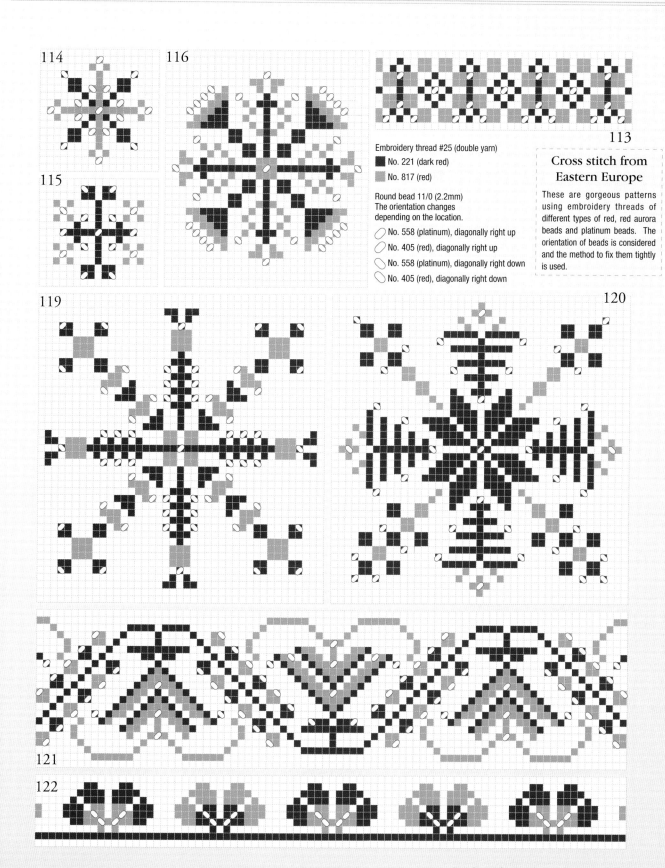

113

Embroidery thread #25 (double yarn)
- ■ No. 221 (dark red)
- ▨ No. 817 (red)

Round bead 11/0 (2.2mm)
The orientation changes
depending on the location.

- ◜ No. 558 (platinum), diagonally right up
- ◝ No. 405 (red), diagonally right up
- ◟ No. 558 (platinum), diagonally right down
- ◞ No. 405 (red), diagonally right down

Cross stitch from Eastern Europe

These are gorgeous patterns using embroidery threads of different types of red, red aurora beads and platinum beads. The orientation of beads is considered and the method to fix them tightly is used.

CROSS STITCH

61

For charts of 117 and 118, please refer to pages 62 - 63.

Basics of cross stitch with beads

Cross stitch, also called counting stitch, is making regular stitches while counting the fabric grain. Upper stitches are normally made in the same direction. However, this direction may be reversed to add a bead in order to emphasize the direction of the bead.

Complete

stitch design
117

Pattern indication

Shows the X of the stitch and ⊘ shows the part to place the beads and the direction. For example…

⊘ Add round bead 8/0 (3.0mm), No. 558 (platinum), diagonally right up.

⊘ Add round bead 8/0 (3.0mm), No. 405 (red), diagonally right down.

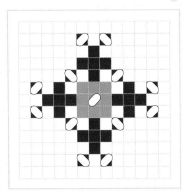

The size of the stitch changes depending on the number of weaving yarns chosen, even if the pattern and the type of fabric are the same.
In the motifs on page 60, 2-yarn stitch to pick up two weaving yarns is used and round beads 11/0 (2.2mm) are added. In the description of the stitching process, 3-yarn stitch is used with round beads 8/0 (3.0mm).

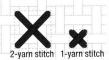

2-yarn stitch 1-yarn stitch

Let's try stitch design 117, an Eastern European stitch.

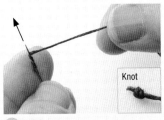

Knot

Complete each X

Stitch each X as you go.

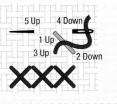

5 Up   4 Down
1 Up
3 Up
2 Down

1 Holding the thread end with the needle, wrap the thread around it a few times. Hold the wrapped part with your finger and pull the needle out.

2 Bring the needle down to the back of the fabric on the point a little way away, and bring the needle up from the back at the starting point. Then finish the end of the thread.

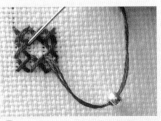

3 Make the stitches around the center bead one by one.

4 Thread a round bead 8/0 (3.0mm) and make a half stitch.

5 Split the 2-yarn thread into half, centering the bead, and make the upper half stitch.

This method is efficient when stitches are continuous or when you want to fill in the surface.

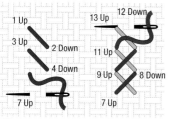

❶ Make half stitches in one direction continuously.

❷ Complete the X as you return.

6 Make half stitches vertically and continuously, then return, forming the remaining halves.

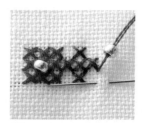

7 When you add beads, stitch each X.

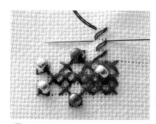

8 Rotate the fabric 90 degrees and make the adjoining part. Note that the direction of the upper thread is changed.

9 Make the four parts in the same manner as ❻-❽.

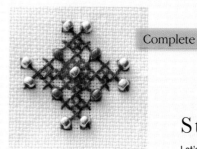

Complete

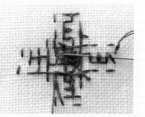

10 Make a knot in the back of the fabric and hide the thread end in the stitched threads. Pull out the starting end to the back of the fabric and finish it in the same way.

Step up

Let's give it a try on a slightly bigger motif!

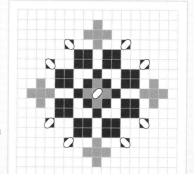

stitch design
118

How to Stitch Seagulls and Palm Trees ▶ P.74

MINI MOTIF
Penguin Family
with Beads

stitch design
123

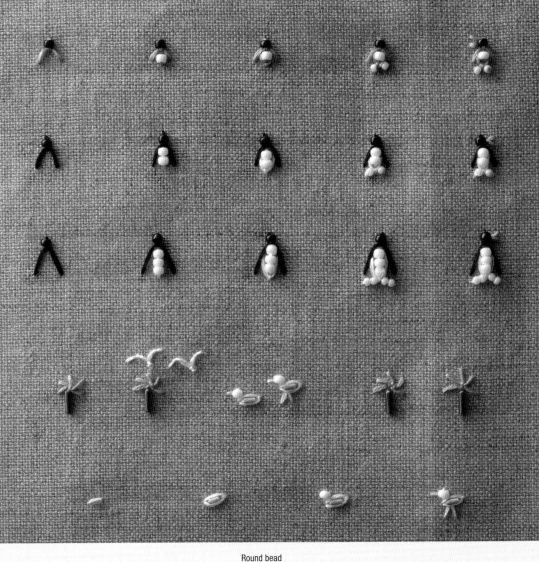

Stitches

Embroidery threads/beads used

Embroidery thread #25/No. 310 (black),
BLANC (white), No. 972 (yellow)/round bead
8/0 (3.0mm) No. 49 (black), No. 121 (white)/
round bead 11/0 (2.2mm) No. 402 (yellow)
*Embroidery threads are made by DMC and
beads are made by TOHO.

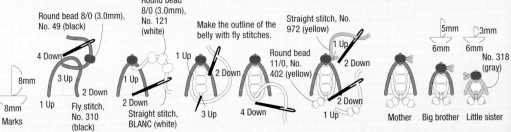

8mm

8mm
Marks

1 Up   2 Down
Fly stitch,
No. 310
(black)

Round bead 8/0 (3.0mm),
No. 49 (black)

4 Down

3 Up

1 Up   2 Down
Straight stitch,
BLANC (white)

Round bead
8/0 (3.0mm),
No. 121
(white)

1 Up
2 Down

Make the outline of the
belly with fly stitches.

1 Up
2 Down

3 Up   4 Down

Round bead
11/0, No.
402 (yellow)

Straight stitch, No.
972 (yellow)

1 Up
2 Down

2 Down
1 Up

5mm
6mm

3mm
6mm

No. 318
(gray)

Mother   Big brother   Little sister

Penguin Family with Beads (123)

How to Stitch with Beads

In this section, we show you how to make cute beaded embroidery stitches via illustrations in an easy-to-understand manner.

Prepare needles, threads, fabrics, your favorite beads and let's get started!

When a special piece is completed, take special care of it so that you can enjoy it for years to come.

Page 14: Sweets Motif Stitch

Embroidery threads/beads used

1   Cup in aqua: No.25 ECRU (natural undyed color, triple yarns) /3mm-long bugle bead 43 (aqua)/round bead 11/0 (2.2mm) 121 (white). Cup in red: No.25 ECRU (natural undyed color, triple yarns)/3mm-long bugle bead 332 (red-purple)/3mm-long bugle bead 121 (white)

2   Pot in aqua: No.25 ECRU (natural undyed color, triple yarns)/3mm-long bugle bead 43 (aqua)/round bead 11/0 (2.2mm) 121 (white)/round bead 8/0 (3.0mm) 403 (aqua). Pot in red: No.25 ECRU (natural undyed color, triple yarns)/3mm-long bugle bead 332 (red-purple)/round bead 11/0 (2.2mm) 121 (white)/round bead 8/0 (3.0mm) 332 (red-purple)

3   Pancakes - Left: No.25 725 (yellow, triple yarns)/round beads 8/0 (3.0mm) & 11/0 (2.2mm) 405 (red). Middle: No.25 725 (yellow, triple yarns), round beads 8/0 (3.0mm) & 11/0 (2.2mm) 332(red-purple), round bead 11/0 (2.2mm) 121 (white). Right: No.25 676 (beige, triple yarns), round beads 8/0 (3.0mm) & 11/0 (2.2mm) 252 (purple)

4   Cakes - Left: No.25 676 (beige, triple yarns)/BLANC (white, double yarns)/round bead 11/0 (2.2mm) 121 (white), 558 (platinum)/round beads 8/0 (3.0mm) 167 (green), 174 (orange), 402 (yellow), 405 (red), 121 (white)/6mm-long bugle bead 332 (red-purple). Right: No.25 676 (beige, triple yarns), 433 (brown, double yarns)/BLANC (white, double yarns)/round bead 11/0 (2.2mm) 121 (white), 332 (red-purple)/round bead 8/0 (3.0mm) 167 (green), 174 (orange), 402 (yellow), 405 (red), 121 (white)/6mm-long bugle bead 111 (orange)

5   Tart: All threads are No.25 676 (beige, triple yarns). Purple: Round bead 8/0 (3.0mm) 252 (purple). Red: Round bead 8/0 (3.0mm) 332 (red-purple). Lime green: 2 round beads 8/0 (3.0mm) 105 (lime green), round bead 8/0 (3.0mm) 174 (orange)

6   Macaroon - Pink: No.25 3689 (pink, triple yarns) ECRU (natural undyed color, triple yarns)/round bead 11/0 (2.2mm) 121 (white). Green: No.25 581 (green, triple yarns), ECRU (natural undyed color, triple yarns)/round bead 11/0 (2.2mm) 121 (white). Yellow: No.25 743 (yellow, triple yarns), ECRU (natural undyed color, triple yarns)/round bead 11/0 (2.2mm) 121 (white).

Shelf   No.5 309 (dark pink, single yarn), No.25 ECRU (natural undyed color, double yarns)/round bead 11/0 (2.2mm) 405 (red)/1.5cm width checkered ribbon

Page 16: Sweets Motif Stitch

Embroidery threads/beads used

7   See page 6-7.

8   Pudding - Left: No.25 725 (yellow, triple yarns), 433 (brown, triple yarns), BLANC (white, triple yarns)/round bead 8/0 (3.0mm) 121 (white), 405 (red)/3mm-long bugle bead 108 (green). Right: No.25 725 (yellow, triple yarns), 433 (brown, triple yarns), BLANC (white, triple yarns)/round bead 8/0 (3.0mm) 121 (white), 332 (red-purple)/round bead 11/0 (2.2mm) 121 (white), 332 (red-purple)

9   Cup cakes - Left: No.25 3822 (yellow, triple yarns), 907 (yellow, triple yarns)/round bead 8/0 (3.0mm) 165 (red), round bead 11/0 (2.2mm) 405 (red). Middle: No.25 605 (pink, triple yarns), BLANC (white, triple yarns)/round bead 8/0 (3.0mm) 332 (red-purple)/round bead 11/0 (2.2mm) 931 (blue). Right: 3822 (yellow, triple yarns), 603 (pink, triple yarns)/round bead 8/0 (3.0mm) 105 (lime green)/round bead 11/0 (2.2mm) 405 (red)

10 Parfait - Left: No.25 BLANC (white, double yarns), 603 (pink, double yarns)/round bead 8/0 (3.0mm) 121 (white), 405 (red)/3mm-long bugle bead 121 (white), 111 (orange). Right: No.25 BLANC (white, double yarns), 827 (aqua, double yarns)/round bead 8/0 (3.0mm) 121 (white), 329 (brown)/3mm-long bugle bead 121 (white), 111 (orange)

11 Cake rolls - Pink: No.25 963 (pink, triple yarns), BLANC (white, double yarns)/round bead 8/0 (3.0mm) 121 (white), 332 (red-purple)/round bead 11/0 (2.2mm) 405 (red), 558 (platinum)/3mm-long bugle bead 121 (white)/6mm-long bugle bead 332 (red-purple). Mocha: No.25 437 (beige, triple yarns), BLANC (white, double yarns)/round bead 8/0 (3.0mm) 174 (orange), 332 (red-purple), 105 (lime green)/round bead 11/0 (2.2mm) 165 (red), 405 (red)/3mm-long bugle bead 121 (white), 6mm-long bugle bead 121 (white). Chocolate: No.25 435 (dark beige, triple yarns), BLANC (white, double yarns)/round bead 8/0 (3.0mm) 121 (white), 405 (red)/round bead 11/0 (2.2mm) 405 (red)/3mm-long bugle bead 121 (white), 6mm-long bugle bead 163 (blue). Bitter: No.25 433 (brown, triple yarns), BLANC (white, double yarns)/round bead 8/0 (3.0mm) 121 (white), 402 (yellow), 405 (red)/round bead 11/0 (2.2mm) 403 (aqua), 405 (red)/3mm-long bugle bead 121 (white), 6mm-long bugle bead 163 (blue).

12 Chair: No.25 800 (aqua, triple yarns/Thread to fix is double yarns), BLANC (white, double yarns), No.5 ECRU (natural undyed color, single yarn)/round bead 11/0 (2.2mm) 403 (aqua)

Table: linen, No.25 BLANC (white, double yarns), ECRU (natural undyed color, single yarn)

Shortcake: No.25 ECRU (natural undyed color, triple yarns), No.8 BLANC (white, single yarn)/round bead 8/0 (3.0mm) 405 (red)/round bead 11/0 (2.2mm) 405 (red), 165 (clear red)

Tip

How to take care of your embroidery items...

After making an item with cute beaded embroidery, wouldn't you prefer to keep it in pristine condition as long as possible? Then be sure to take special care of it, handling the beads and base fabrics carefully.

To clean the item, hand-wash gently after turning it inside-out so that the beaded surface is inside. When using a washing machine, make sure the item is placed in a cleaning net.

To air dry the item, make sure that the beaded surface is on the inside and air it in the shade to prevent discoloration of the beads.

Washing is not recommended for some beads and spangles, so don't forget to check the instructions before using!

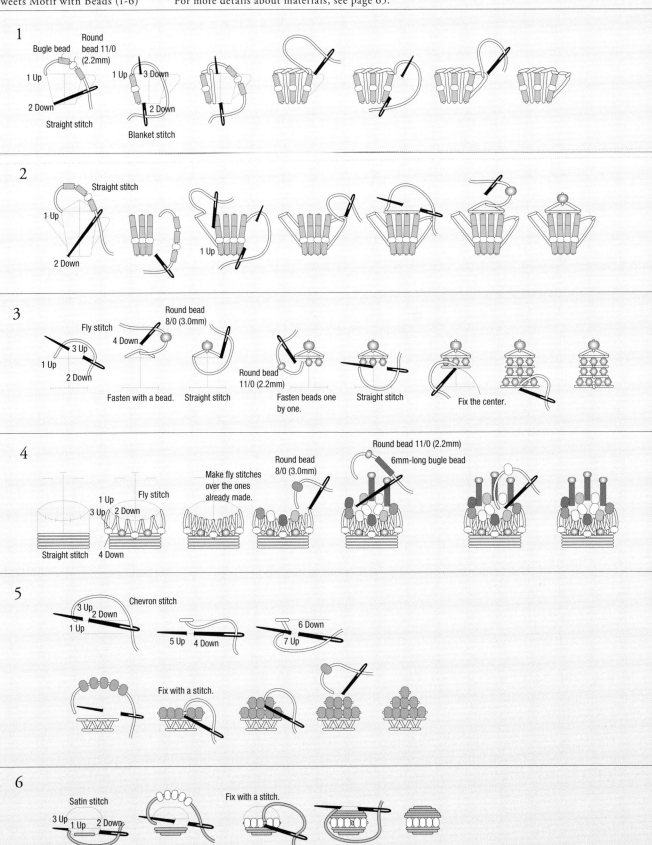

1

Bugle bead Round bead 11/0 (2.2mm)
1 Up
2 Down
Straight stitch
1 Up 3 Down
2 Down
Blanket stitch

2

Straight stitch
1 Up
2 Down
1 Up

3

Fly stitch
Round bead 8/0 (3.0mm)
3 Up 4 Down
1 Up
2 Down
Fasten with a bead. Straight stitch
Round bead 11/0 (2.2mm)
Fasten beads one by one. Straight stitch
Fix the center.

4

1 Up Fly stitch
3 Up 2 Down
Straight stitch 4 Down
Make fly stitches over the ones already made.
Round bead 8/0 (3.0mm)
Round bead 11/0 (2.2mm)
6mm-long bugle bead

5

3 Up 2 Down Chevron stitch
1 Up
5 Up 4 Down
6 Down
7 Up
Fix with a stitch.

6

Satin stitch
3 Up 1 Up 2 Down
Fix with a stitch.

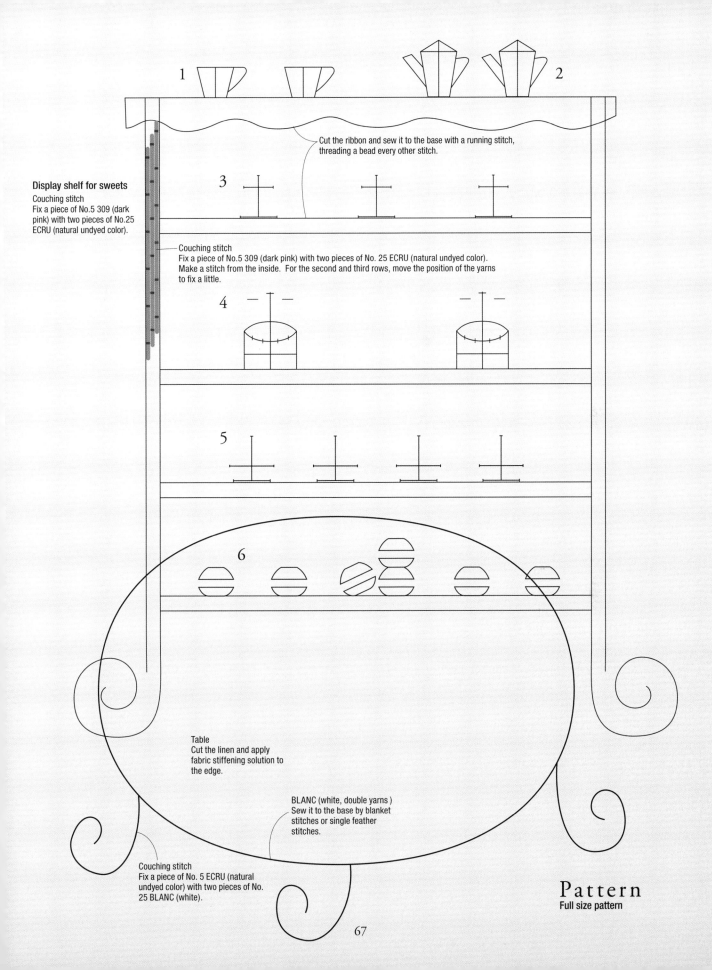

1

2

Cut the ribbon and sew it to the base with a running stitch, threading a bead every other stitch.

Display shelf for sweets
Couching stitch
Fix a piece of No.5 309 (dark pink) with two pieces of No.25 ECRU (natural undyed color).

3

Couching stitch
Fix a piece of No.5 309 (dark pink) with two pieces of No. 25 ECRU (natural undyed color).
Make a stitch from the inside. For the second and third rows, move the position of the yarns to fix a little.

4

5

6

Table
Cut the linen and apply fabric stiffening solution to the edge.

BLANC (white, double yarns)
Sew it to the base by blanket stitches or single feather stitches.

Couching stitch
Fix a piece of No. 5 ECRU (natural undyed color) with two pieces of No. 25 BLANC (white).

Pattern
Full size pattern

8

★ Change thread. Make the caramel sauce part with brown embroidery thread (2 rows).

Full size pattern

Make satin stitches with yellow embroidery thread (5 rows).

Make a topping with your favorite beads.

Make stitches for a plate, referring to the instructions for shortcake.

9

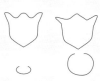

Full size pattern

Make the icing with Romanian stitches.

1 Up 3 Up 2 Down
5 Up 4 Down

Round bead 8/0 (3.0mm)

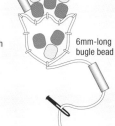
Make the cup part with Blanket stitches.

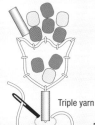
Round bead 11/0 (2.2mm)

12

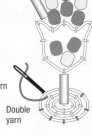

Full size pattern

Couching stitch
For the seat part, make a stitch, threading a bead every other stitch.

10

Full size pattern

Use 3mm-long bugle beads for the work in page 16.
Personalize it with your favorite beads!

Core thread (triple yarns)

1 Up 2 Down

Couching stitch

Thread for fixing (double yarns)

6mm-long bugle bead

Triple yarn

Double yarn

11

Full size pattern

Make chain stitches according to the pattern from the inside.

Camouflage the thread end with chains.

Insert your favorite beads in between the lines of the spiral.

P.4 Shortcakes

Fly stitch
4 Down
1 Up 3 Up 2 Down

Full size pattern

5 Up 6 Down
Straight stitch

Round bead 8/0 (3.0mm)

Width of a round bead 8/0 (3.0mm)
Cross the thread of the fly stitch

Make the sponge part.

Fasten 4 beads in the same manner as making a running stitch.

Make the second row of straight stitches as if round beads 11/0 (2.2mm) are sandwiched within the two rows of stitches.

Add another row of stitches and beads

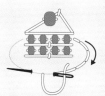
Make backstitches for the perimeter of the cake.

Bring the needle up from the back.

Pass another thread through the backstitches to make a lace paper doily.

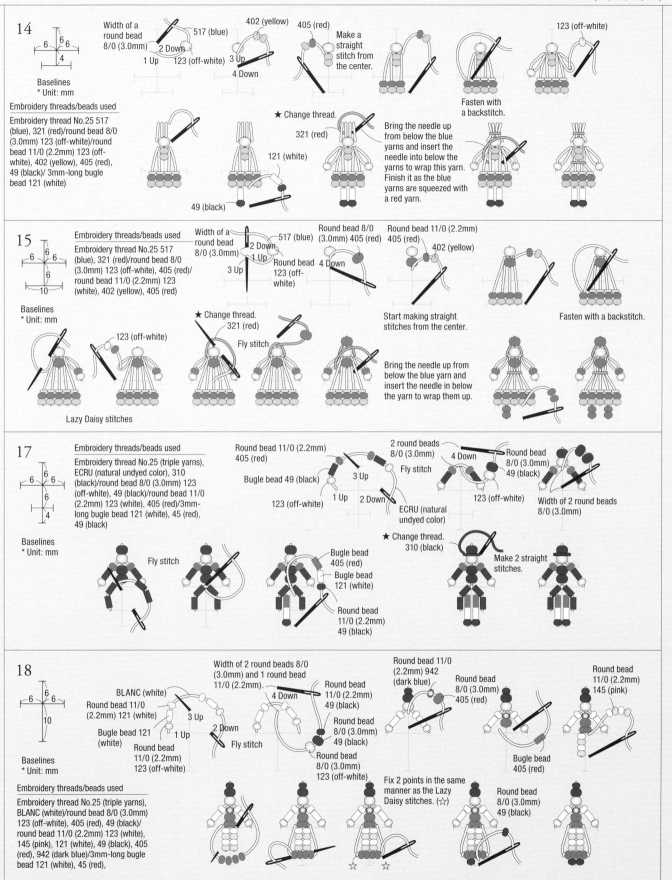

14

6 6 6
     4

Baselines
* Unit: mm

Embroidery threads/beads used

Embroidery thread No.25 517 (blue), 321 (red)/round bead 8/0 (3.0mm) 123 (off-white)/round bead 11/0 (2.2mm) 123 (off-white), 402 (yellow), 405 (red), 49 (black)/ 3mm-long bugle bead 121 (white)

Width of a round bead 8/0 (3.0mm)
517 (blue)
402 (yellow)
405 (red)
2 Down
1 Up   123 (off-white)
3 Up
4 Down
Make a straight stitch from the center.
123 (off-white)
Fasten with a backstitch.

★ Change thread.
321 (red)
121 (white)
49 (black)

Bring the needle up from below the blue yarns and insert the needle into below the yarns to wrap this yarn. Finish it as the blue yarns are squeezed with a red yarn.

15

6 6 6
     6
6   10

Baselines
* Unit: mm

Embroidery threads/beads used

Embroidery thread No.25 517 (blue), 321 (red)/round bead 8/0 (3.0mm) 123 (off-white), 405 (red)/ round bead 11/0 (2.2mm) 123 (white), 402 (yellow), 405 (red)

Width of a round bead 8/0 (3.0mm)
2 Down
1 Up
3 Up
517 (blue)
Round bead 123 (off-white)
Round bead 8/0 (3.0mm) 405 (red)
Round bead 11/0 (2.2mm) 405 (red)
402 (yellow)
4 Down
Start making straight stitches from the center.
Fasten with a backstitch.

★ Change thread.
321 (red)
Fly stitch
123 (off-white)

Bring the needle up from below the blue yarn and insert the needle in below the yarn to wrap them up.

Lazy Daisy stitches.

17

6 6 6
     6
     4

Baselines
* Unit: mm

Embroidery threads/beads used

Embroidery thread No.25 (triple yarns), ECRU (natural undyed color), 310 (black)/round bead 8/0 (3.0mm) 123 (off-white), 49 (black)/round bead 11/0 (2.2mm) 123 (white), 405 (red)/3mm-long bugle bead 121 (white), 45 (red), 49 (black)

Round bead 11/0 (2.2mm) 405 (red)
2 round beads 8/0 (3.0mm)
4 Down
Round bead 8/0 (3.0mm) 49 (black)
Bugle bead 49 (black)
3 Up
Fly stitch
1 Up   2 Down
123 (off-white)
ECRU (natural undyed color)
123 (off-white)
Width of 2 round beads 8/0 (3.0mm)

★ Change thread.
310 (black)
Make 2 straight stitches.

Fly stitch

Bugle bead 405 (red)
Bugle bead 121 (white)
Round bead 11/0 (2.2mm) 49 (black)

18

6 6 6
     10

Baselines
* Unit: mm

Embroidery threads/beads used

Embroidery thread No.25 (triple yarns), BLANC (white)/round bead 8/0 (3.0mm) 123 (off-white), 405 (red), 49 (black)/ round bead 11/0 (2.2mm) 123 (white), 145 (pink), 121 (white), 49 (black), 405 (red), 942 (dark blue)/3mm-long bugle bead 121 (white), 45 (red),

BLANC (white)
Round bead 11/0 (2.2mm) 121 (white)
Bugle bead 121 (white)
Round bead 11/0 (2.2mm) 123 (off-white)
Width of 2 round beads 8/0 (3.0mm) and 1 round bead 11/0 (2.2mm).
3 Up
2 Down
1 Up
Fly stitch
4 Down
Round bead 11/0 (2.2mm) 49 (black)
Round bead 8/0 (3.0mm) 49 (black)
Round bead 8/0 (3.0mm) 123 (off-white)
Round bead 11/0 (2.2mm) 942 (dark blue)
Round bead 8/0 (3.0mm) 405 (red)
Round bead 11/0 (2.2mm) 145 (pink)
Bugle bead 405 (red)

Fix 2 points in the same manner as the Lazy Daisy stitches. (☆)

Round bead 8/0 (3.0mm) 49 (black)

☆ ☆

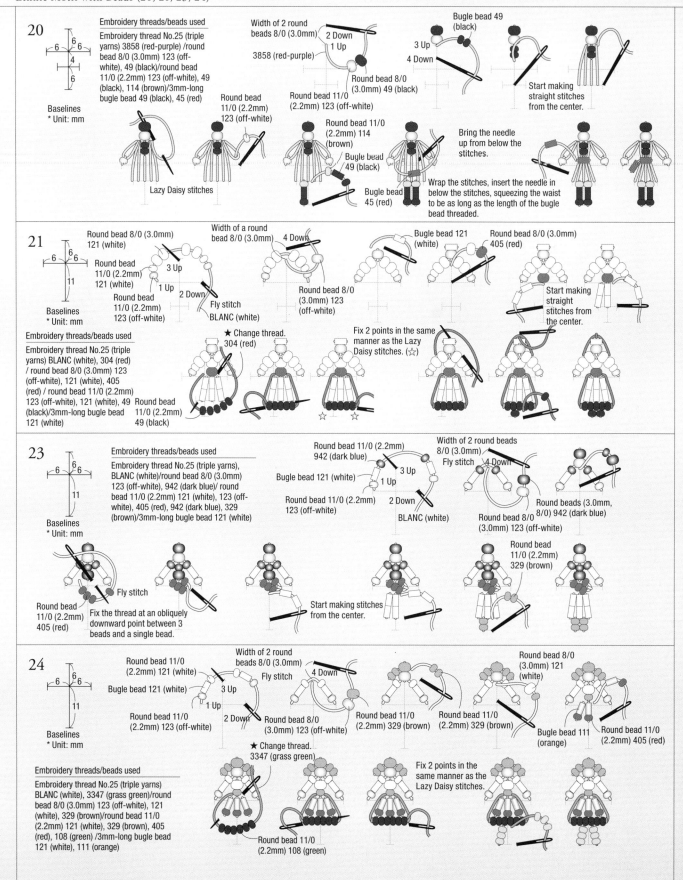

20

Baselines
* Unit: mm

6 6
4
6

Embroidery threads/beads used

Embroidery thread No.25 (triple yarns) 3858 (red-purple) /round bead 8/0 (3.0mm) 123 (off-white), 49 (black)/round bead 11/0 (2.2mm) 123 (off-white), 49 (black), 114 (brown)/3mm-long bugle bead 49 (black), 45 (red)

Width of 2 round beads 8/0 (3.0mm)
2 Down
1 Up
3858 (red-purple)
Round bead 8/0 (3.0mm) 49 (black)
Round bead 11/0 (2.2mm) 123 (off-white)

Bugle bead 49 (black)
3 Up
4 Down

Start making straight stitches from the center.

Round bead 11/0 (2.2mm) 123 (off-white)
Lazy Daisy stitches

Round bead 11/0 (2.2mm) 114 (brown)
Bugle bead 49 (black)
Bugle bead 45 (red)

Bring the needle up from below the stitches.

Wrap the stitches, insert the needle in below the stitches, squeezing the waist to be as long as the length of the bugle bead threaded.

21

Baselines
* Unit: mm

6 6
6
11

Embroidery threads/beads used

Embroidery thread No.25 (triple yarns) BLANC (white), 304 (red) / round bead 8/0 (3.0mm) 123 (off-white), 121 (white), 405 (red) / round bead 11/0 (2.2mm) 123 (off-white), 121 (white), 49 (black)/3mm-long bugle bead 121 (white)

Round bead 8/0 (3.0mm) 121 (white)
Round bead 11/0 (2.2mm) 121 (white)
3 Up
1 Up
2 Down
Round bead 11/0 (2.2mm) 123 (off-white)
Fly stitch BLANC (white)

Width of a round bead 8/0 (3.0mm)
4 Down
Round bead 8/0 (3.0mm) 123 (off-white)

Bugle bead 121 (white)
Round bead 8/0 (3.0mm) 405 (red)

Start making straight stitches from the center.

★ Change thread. 304 (red)

Round bead 11/0 (2.2mm) 49 (black)

Fix 2 points in the same manner as the Lazy Daisy stitches. (☆)
☆ ☆

23

Baselines
* Unit: mm

6 6
11

Embroidery threads/beads used

Embroidery thread No.25 (triple yarns), BLANC (white)/round bead 8/0 (3.0mm) 123 (off-white), 942 (dark blue)/ round bead 11/0 (2.2mm) 121 (white), 123 (off-white), 405 (red), 942 (dark blue), 329 (brown)/3mm-long bugle bead 121 (white)

Round bead 11/0 (2.2mm) 942 (dark blue)
Bugle bead 121 (white)
3 Up
1 Up
2 Down
Round bead 11/0 (2.2mm) 123 (off-white)
BLANC (white)

Width of 2 round beads 8/0 (3.0mm)
Fly stitch 4 Down
Round bead 8/0 (3.0mm) 123 (off-white)
Round beads (3.0mm, 8/0) 942 (dark blue)

Round bead 11/0 (2.2mm) 405 (red)
Fly stitch
Fix the thread at an obliquely downward point between 3 beads and a single bead.

Start making stitches from the center.

Round bead 11/0 (2.2mm) 329 (brown)

24

Baselines
* Unit: mm

6 6
11

Embroidery threads/beads used

Embroidery thread No.25 (triple yarns) BLANC (white), 3347 (grass green)/round bead 8/0 (3.0mm) 123 (off-white), 121 (white), 329 (brown)/round bead 11/0 (2.2mm) 121 (white), 329 (brown), 405 (red), 108 (green) /3mm-long bugle bead 121 (white), 111 (orange)

Round bead 11/0 (2.2mm) 121 (white)
Bugle bead 121 (white)
3 Up
1 Up
2 Down
Round bead 11/0 (2.2mm) 123 (off-white)

Width of 2 round beads 8/0 (3.0mm)
Fly stitch
4 Down
Round bead 8/0 (3.0mm) 123 (off-white)
Round bead 11/0 (2.2mm) 329 (brown)
Round bead 11/0 (2.2mm) 329 (brown)

Round bead 8/0 (3.0mm) 121 (white)
Bugle bead 111 (orange)
Round bead 11/0 (2.2mm) 405 (red)

★ Change thread. 3347 (grass green)

Round bead 11/0 (2.2mm) 108 (green)

Fix 2 points in the same manner as the Lazy Daisy stitches.

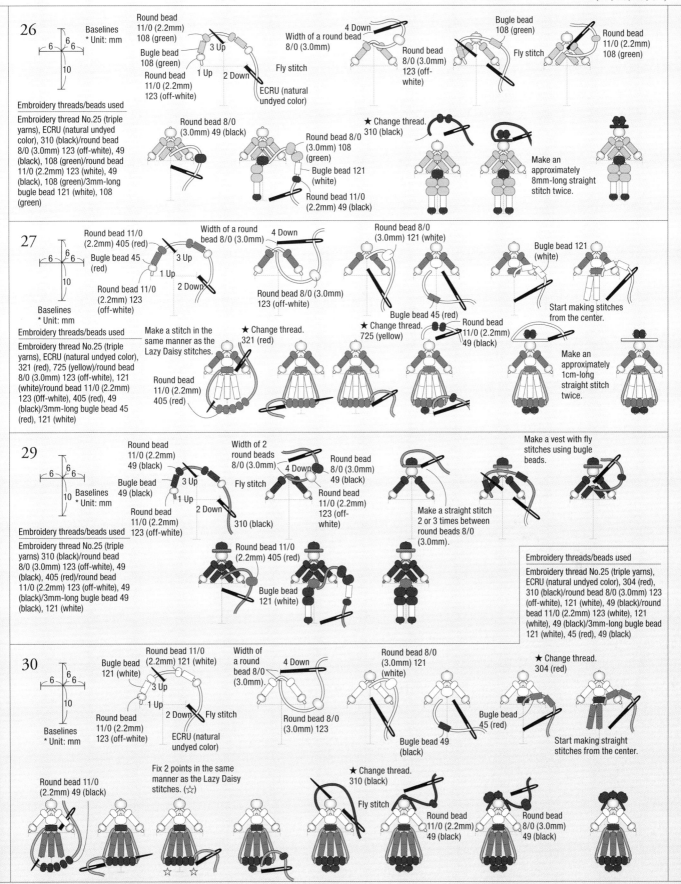

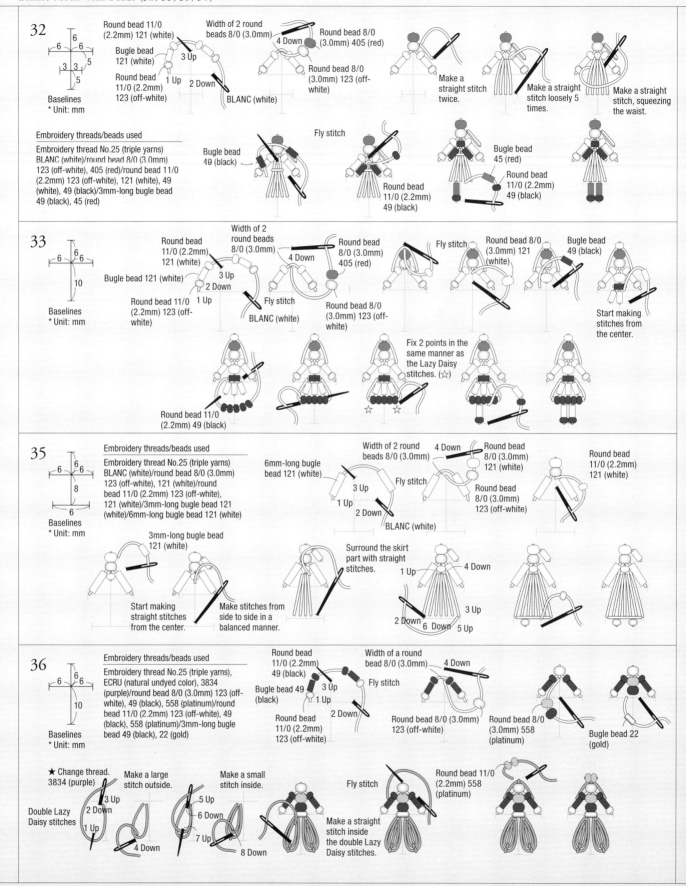

32

Baselines
* Unit: mm

Round bead 11/0 (2.2mm) 121 (white)
Bugle bead 121 (white)
Round bead 11/0 (2.2mm) 123 (off-white)
Width of 2 round beads 8/0 (3.0mm)
4 Down
3 Up
1 Up
2 Down
BLANC (white)
Round bead 8/0 (3.0mm) 405 (red)
Round bead 8/0 (3.0mm) 123 (off-white)
Make a straight stitch twice.
Make a straight stitch loosely 5 times.
Make a straight stitch, squeezing the waist.

Embroidery threads/beads used
Embroidery thread No.25 (triple yarns) BLANC (white)/round bead 8/0 (3.0mm) 123 (off-red), 405 (red)/round bead 11/0 (2.2mm) 123 (off-white), 121 (white), 49 (white), 49 (black)/3mm-long bugle bead 49 (black), 45 (red)

Fly stitch
Bugle bead 49 (black)
Round bead 11/0 (2.2mm) 49 (black)
Bugle bead 45 (red)
Round bead 11/0 (2.2mm) 49 (black)

33

Baselines
* Unit: mm

Round bead 11/0 (2.2mm) 121 (white)
Bugle bead 121 (white)
Round bead 11/0 (2.2mm) 123 (off-white)
Width of 2 round beads 8/0 (3.0mm)
4 Down
3 Up
2 Down
1 Up
Fly stitch
BLANC (white)
Round bead 8/0 (3.0mm) 405 (red)
Round bead 8/0 (3.0mm) 123 (off-white)
Fly stitch
Round bead 8/0 (3.0mm) 121 (white)
Bugle bead 49 (black)
Start making stitches from the center.

Round bead 11/0 (2.2mm) 49 (black)
Fix 2 points in the same manner as the Lazy Daisy stitches. (☆)

35

Baselines
* Unit: mm

Embroidery threads/beads used
Embroidery thread No.25 (triple yarns) BLANC (white)/round bead 8/0 (3.0mm) 123 (off-white), 121 (white)/round bead 11/0 (2.2mm) 123 (off-white), 121 (white)/3mm-long bugle bead 121 (white)/6mm-long bugle bead 121 (white)

6mm-long bugle bead 121 (white)
Width of 2 round beads 8/0 (3.0mm)
4 Down
3 Up
1 Up
2 Down
Fly stitch
BLANC (white)
Round bead 8/0 (3.0mm) 121 (white)
Round bead 8/0 (3.0mm) 123 (off-white)
Round bead 11/0 (2.2mm) 121 (white)

3mm-long bugle bead 121 (white)
Start making straight stitches from the center.
Make stitches from side to side in a balanced manner.
Surround the skirt part with straight stitches.
1 Up
4 Down
3 Up
2 Down
6 Down
5 Up

36

Baselines
* Unit: mm

Embroidery threads/beads used
Embroidery thread No.25 (triple yarns), ECRU (natural undyed color), 3834 (purple)/round bead 8/0 (3.0mm) 123 (off-white), 49 (black), 558 (platinum)/round bead 11/0 (2.2mm) 123 (off-white), 49 (black), 558 (platinum)/3mm-long bugle bead 49 (black), 22 (gold)

Round bead 11/0 (2.2mm) 49 (black)
Bugle bead 49 (black)
Round bead 11/0 (2.2mm) 123 (off-white)
3 Up
1 Up
2 Down
Width of a round bead 8/0 (3.0mm)
4 Down
Fly stitch
Round bead 8/0 (3.0mm) 123 (off-white)
Round bead 8/0 (3.0mm) 558 (platinum)
Bugle bead 22 (gold)
Round bead 11/0 (2.2mm) 558 (platinum)

★ Change thread. 3834 (purple)
Double Lazy Daisy stitches
Make a large stitch outside.
3 Up
2 Down
1 Up
4 Down
Make a small stitch inside.
5 Up
6 Down
7 Up
8 Down
Fly stitch
Make a straight stitch inside the double Lazy Daisy stitches.

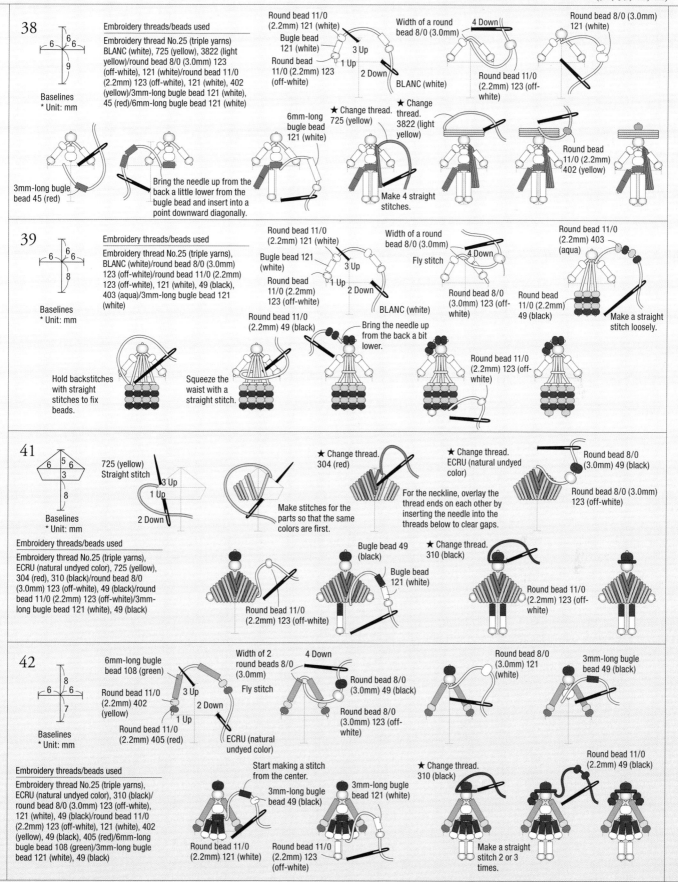

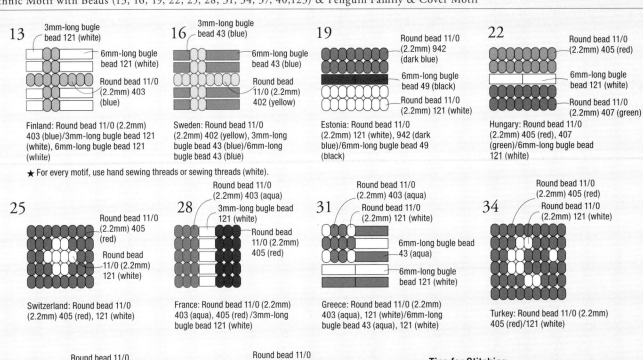

13 — 3mm-long bugle bead 121 (white) / 6mm-long bugle bead 121 (white) / Round bead 11/0 (2.2mm) 403 (blue)

Finland: Round bead 11/0 (2.2mm) 403 (blue)/3mm-long bugle bead 121 (white), 6mm-long bugle bead 121 (white)

16 — 3mm-long bugle bead 43 (blue) / 6mm-long bugle bead 43 (blue) / Round bead 11/0 (2.2mm) 402 (yellow)

Sweden: Round bead 11/0 (2.2mm) 402 (yellow), 3mm-long bugle bead 43 (blue)/6mm-long bugle bead 43 (blue)

19 — Round bead 11/0 (2.2mm) 942 (dark blue) / 6mm-long bugle bead 49 (black) / Round bead 11/0 (2.2mm) 121 (white)

Estonia: Round bead 11/0 (2.2mm) 121 (white), 942 (dark blue)/6mm-long bugle bead 49 (black)

22 — Round bead 11/0 (2.2mm) 405 (red) / 6mm-long bugle bead 121 (white) / Round bead 11/0 (2.2mm) 407 (green)

Hungary: Round bead 11/0 (2.2mm) 405 (red), 407 (green)/6mm-long bugle bead 121 (white)

★ For every motif, use hand sewing threads or sewing threads (white).

25 — Round bead 11/0 (2.2mm) 405 (red) / Round bead 11/0 (2.2mm) 121 (white)

Switzerland: Round bead 11/0 (2.2mm) 405 (red), 121 (white)

28 — Round bead 11/0 (2.2mm) 403 (aqua) / 3mm-long bugle bead 121 (white) / Round bead 11/0 (2.2mm) 405 (red)

France: Round bead 11/0 (2.2mm) 403 (aqua), 405 (red) /3mm-long bugle bead 121 (white)

31 — Round bead 11/0 (2.2mm) 403 (aqua) / Round bead 11/0 (2.2mm) 121 (white) / 6mm-long bugle bead 43 (aqua) / 6mm-long bugle bead 121 (white)

Greece: Round bead 11/0 (2.2mm) 403 (aqua), 121 (white)/6mm-long bugle bead 43 (aqua), 121 (white)

34 — Round bead 11/0 (2.2mm) 405 (red) / Round bead 11/0 (2.2mm) 121 (white)

Turkey: Round bead 11/0 (2.2mm) 405 (red)/121 (white)

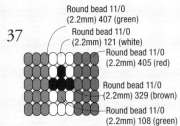

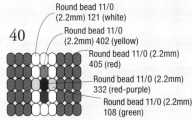

37 — Round bead 11/0 (2.2mm) 407 (green) / Round bead 11/0 (2.2mm) 121 (white) / Round bead 11/0 (2.2mm) 405 (red) / Round bead 11/0 (2.2mm) 329 (brown) / Round bead 11/0 (2.2mm) 108 (green)

Mexico: Round bead 11/0 (2.2mm) 405 (red), 121 (white), 407 (green), 108 (green), 329 (brown)

40 — Round bead 11/0 (2.2mm) 121 (white) / Round bead 11/0 (2.2mm) 402 (yellow) / Round bead 11/0 (2.2mm) 405 (red) / Round bead 11/0 (2.2mm) 332 (red-purple) / Round bead 11/0 (2.2mm) 108 (green)

Peru: Round bead 11/0 (2.2mm) 405 (red), 121 (white), 402 (yellow), 332 (red-purple), 108 (green)

Tips for Stitching

- Start by bringing the needle up from the back, making 2 or 3 small stitches, then bring the needle up again from the back at the starting point.

- Thread beads for 1 row, then make a stitch in the same way as a straight stitch, being careful not to create gaps.

- Finally, fix the center with a stitch so it is not noticeable.

- At the end, make 2 or 3 small stitches in order to not show the seam, make a knot, then cut the thread.

123   Seagulls and Palm Trees

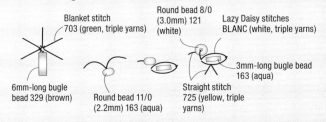

Blanket stitch 703 (green, triple yarns) / Round bead 8/0 (3.0mm) 121 (white) / Lazy Daisy stitches BLANC (white, triple yarns) / 3mm-long bugle bead 163 (aqua) / 6mm-long bugle bead 329 (brown) / Round bead 11/0 (2.2mm) 163 (aqua) / Straight stitch 725 (yellow, triple yarns)

P.64 Penguin Family mini Motif Stitch
Embroidery threads/beads used

123 No.25 BLANC (white, triple yarns), 725 (yellow, triple yarns), 703 (green, triple yarns)/round bead 8/0 (3.0mm) 121 (white)/round bead 11/0 (2.2mm) 163 (aqua)/3mm-long bugle bead 163 (aqua), 6mm-long bugle bead 329 (brown)

50

51

52

Pattern

Pattern reduced to 87% <Enlarge to 115% to use.>

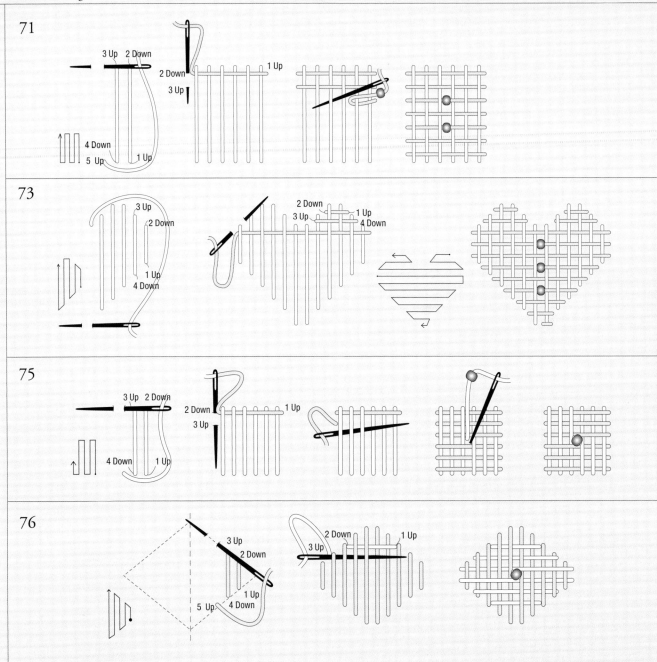

Page 46: Surface Darning Stitch
Embroidery threads/beads used

71 123 No.25 BLANC (white, triple yarns), 725 (yellow, triple yarns), 703 (green, triple yarns)/round bead 8/0 (3.0mm) 121 (white)/round bead 11/0 (2.2mm) 163 (aqua)/3mm-long bugle bead 163 (aqua), 6mm-long bugle bead 329 (brown)

72 Embroidery Thread No.5 single yarn 975 (brown), 782 (ocher), 437 (beige)/round bead 8/0 (3.0mm) 405 (red), 105 (lime green), 332 (red-purple), 165 (red)

73 Embroidery Thread No.5 single yarn 975 (brown), 782 (ocher), 437 (beige), ECRU (natural undyed color)/round bead 8/0 (3.0mm) 105 (lime green), 332 (red-purple), 405 (red)

74 Embroidery Thread No.5 single yarn 975 (brown), 782 (ocher), 437 (beige)/round bead 8/0 (3.0mm) 401 (white), 405 (red), 332 (red-purple)

75 Embroidery Thread No.5 single yarn 975 (brown), 782 (ocher), 437 (beige)/round bead 8/0 (3.0mm) 557 (gold), 332 (red-purple)

76 Embroidery Thread No.5 single yarn 975 (brown), 782 (ocher), 437 (beige)/round bead 8/0 (3.0mm) 105 (lime green), 332 (red-purple)

77 Embroidery Thread No.5 single yarn 975 (brown), 782 (ocher), 437 (beige)/round bead 8/0 (3.0mm) 165 (red), 105 (ocher), 332 (red-purple)

78 Embroidery Thread No.5 single yarn 975 (brown), 782 (ocher)/round bead 8/0 (3.0mm) 332 (red-purple), 405 (red)

72

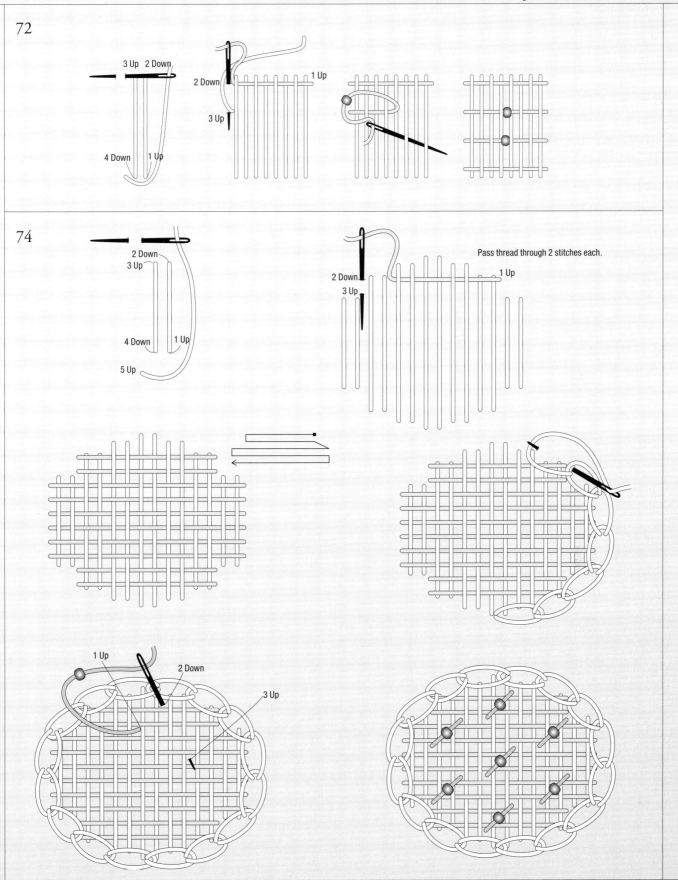

3 Up 2 Down

2 Down 1 Up

3 Up

4 Down 1 Up

74

2 Down
3 Up

4 Down 1 Up

5 Up

2 Down 1 Up
3 Up

Pass thread through 2 stitches each.

1 Up 2 Down

3 Up

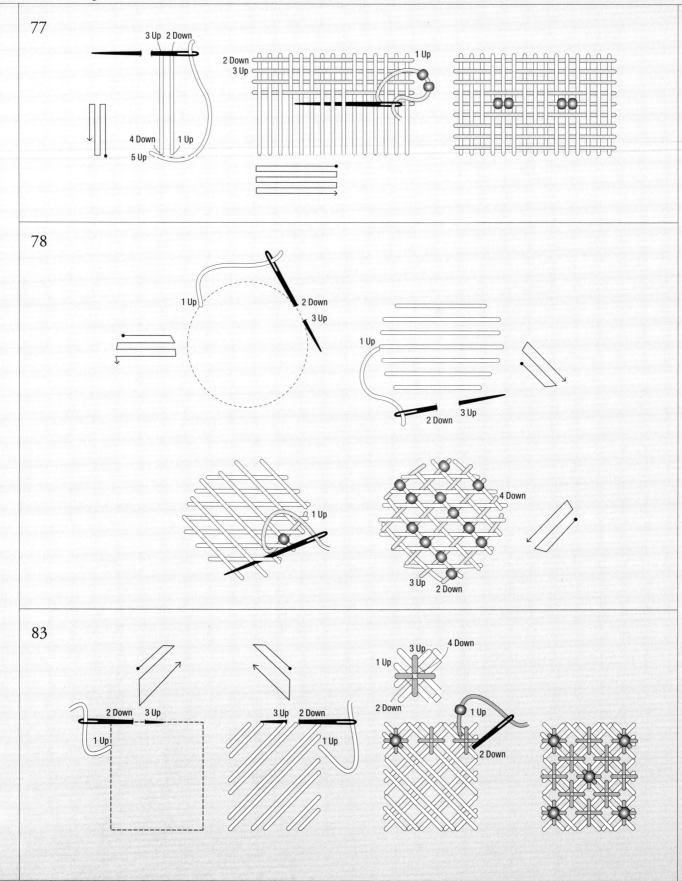

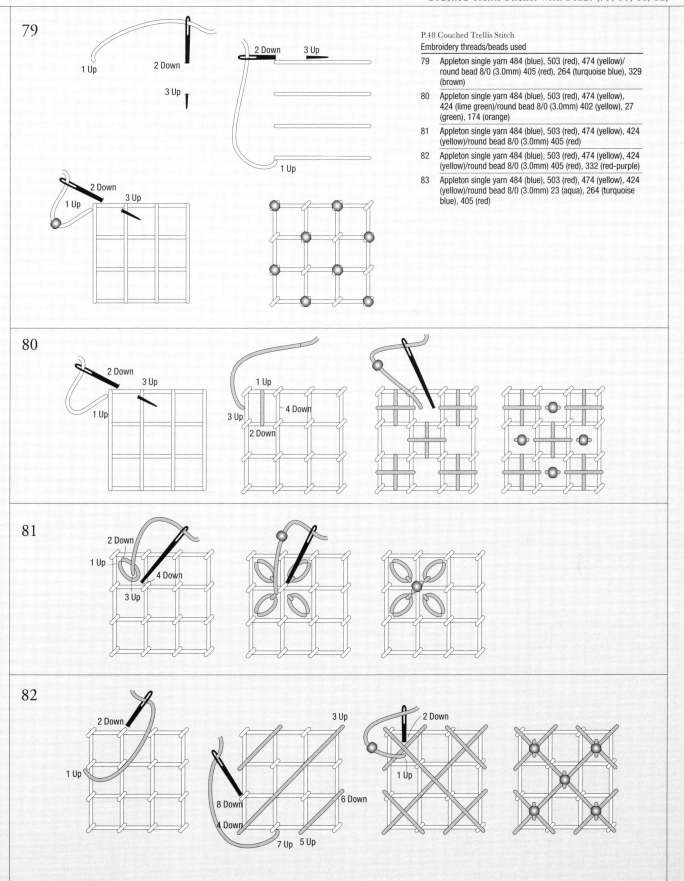

P.48 Couched Trellis Stitch
Embroidery threads/beads used

79 Appleton single yarn 484 (blue), 503 (red), 474 (yellow)/
round bead 8/0 (3.0mm) 405 (red), 264 (turquoise blue), 329
(brown)

80 Appleton single yarn 484 (blue), 503 (red), 474 (yellow),
424 (lime green)/round bead 8/0 (3.0mm) 402 (yellow), 27
(green), 174 (orange)

81 Appleton single yarn 484 (blue), 503 (red), 474 (yellow), 424
(yellow)/round bead 8/0 (3.0mm) 405 (red)

82 Appleton single yarn 484 (blue), 503 (red), 474 (yellow), 424
(yellow)/round bead 8/0 (3.0mm) 405 (red), 332 (red-purple)

83 Appleton single yarn 484 (blue), 503 (red), 474 (yellow), 424
(yellow)/round bead 8/0 (3.0mm) 23 (aqua), 264 (turquoise
blue), 405 (red)

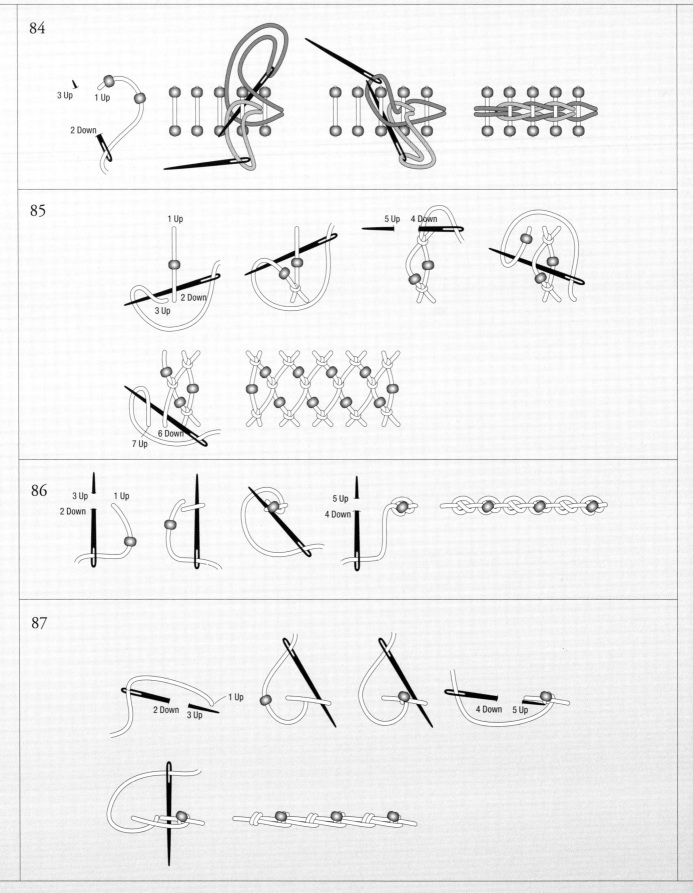

84

85

86

87

88

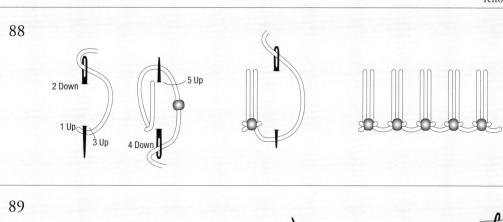

89

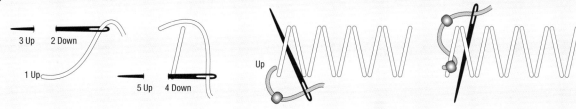

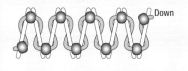

P.50 Knotted Stitch
Embroidery threads/beads used

84	Appleton double yarns 223 (pink), 227 (dark pink)/round bead 8/0 (3.0mm) 905 (pink), 332 (red-purple), 405 (red), 169 (light pink), 31 (pink)
85	Appleton double yarns 221 (pink)/round bead 8/0 (3.0mm) 332 (red-purple), 31 (pink), 905 (pink), 557 (gold), 169 (light pink)
86	Appleton double yarns 222 (pink)/round bead 8/0 (3.0mm) 557 (gold), 332 (red purple)
87	Appleton double yarns 223 (pink)/round bead 8/0 (3.0mm) 405 (red), 31 (pink), 905 (pink)
88	Appleton double yarns 225 (pink)/round bead 8/0 (3.0mm) 559 (gold), 905 (pink), 332 (red-purple)
89	Appleton double yarns 226 (dark pink), 222 (pink)/round bead 8/0 (3.0mm) 332 (red-purple), 31 (pink), 123 (off-white)
90	Appleton double yarns 223 (pink), 227 (dark pink)/round bead 8/0 (3.0mm) 31 (pink)

P.52 Darning Stitch
Embroidery threads/beads used

91	No. 5 single yarn 420 (dark beige), 841 (beige), 842 (light beige)/round bead 8/0 (3.0mm) 122 (milk white), 105 (lime green), 162 (light brown)
92	No. 5 single yarn 420 (dark beige), 841 (beige), 842 (light beige)/round bead 8/0 (3.0mm) 123 (off white), 105 (lime green)
93	No. 5 single yarn 420 (dark beige), 841 (beige), 842 (light beige)/6mm-long bugle bead 122 (milk white), 22 (gold), 44 (lime green), 167 (green)
94	No. 5 single yarn 420 (dark beige), 841 (beige), 842 (light beige)/6mm-long bugle bead 122 (milk white), 22 (gold), 44 (lime green), 167 (green)
95	No. 5 single yarn 420 (dark beige), 841 (beige), 842 (light beige)/6mm-long bugle bead 167 (green), 22 (gold), 44 (lime green)
96	No. 5 single yarn 420 (dark beige), 841 (beige), 842 (light beige)/round bead 8/0 (3.0mm) 122 (milk white), 105 (lime green), 162 (light brown)

90

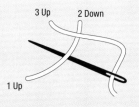

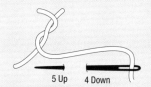

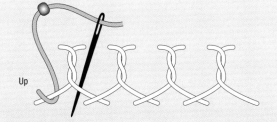

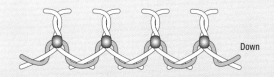

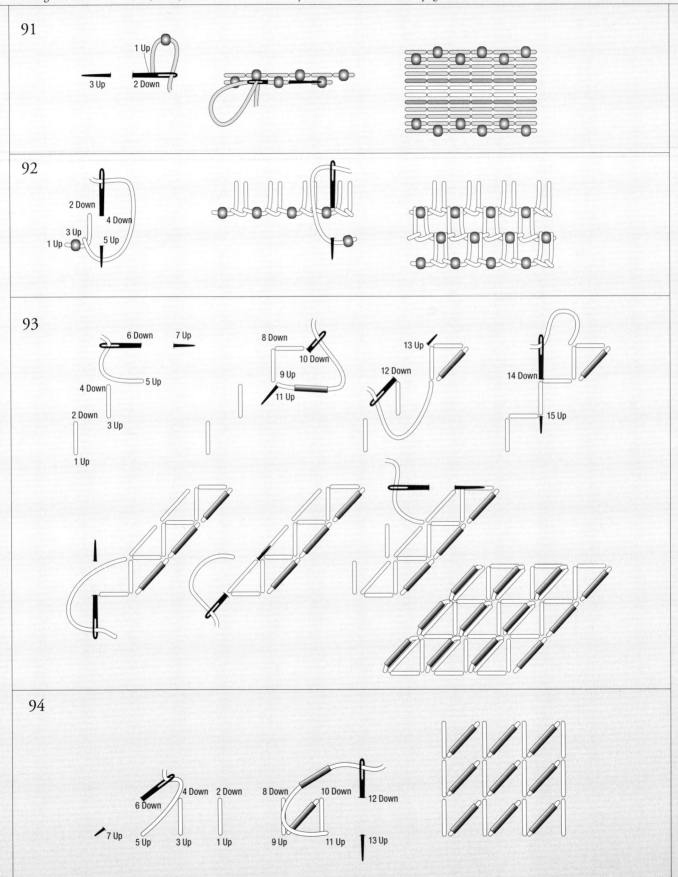

91

3 Up   1 Up   2 Down

92

2 Down   4 Down   3 Up   1 Up   5 Up

93

6 Down   7 Up   8 Down   10 Down   13 Up
4 Down   5 Up   9 Up   12 Down   14 Down   15 Up
2 Down   3 Up   11 Up
1 Up

94

6 Down   4 Down   2 Down   8 Down   10 Down   12 Down
7 Up   5 Up   3 Up   1 Up   9 Up   11 Up   13 Up

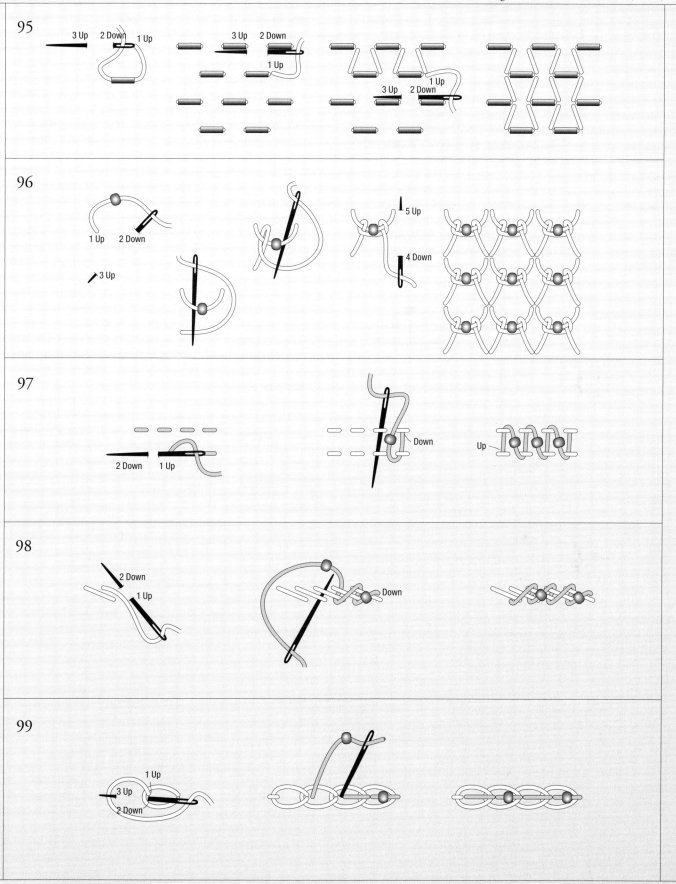

95

3 Up   2 Down   1 Up

3 Up   2 Down

1 Up

3 Up   2 Down

1 Up

96

1 Up   2 Down

3 Up

5 Up

4 Down

97

2 Down   1 Up

Down

Up

98

2 Down

1 Up

Down

99

1 Up

3 Up

2 Down

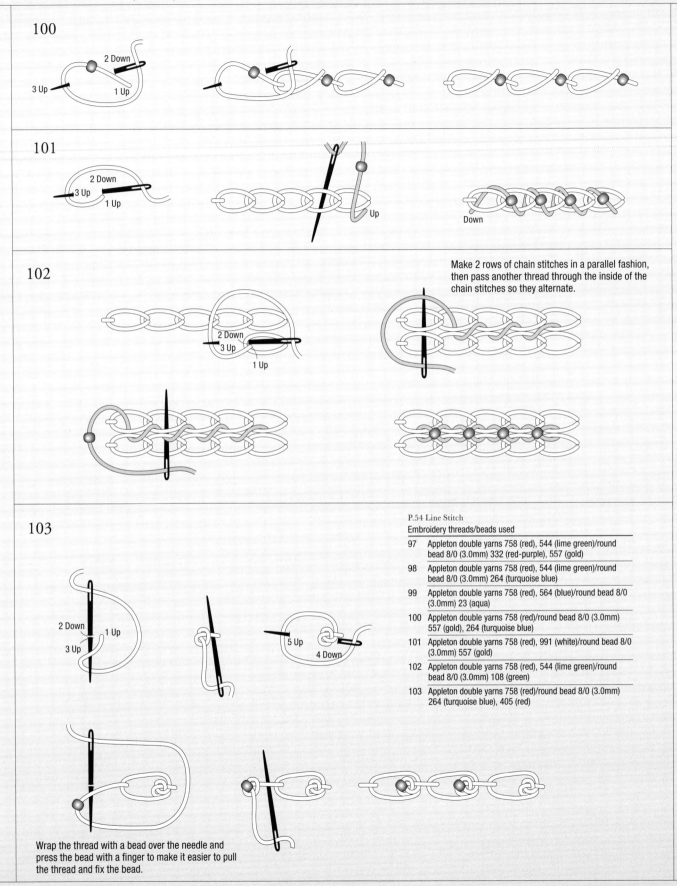

100

3 Up / 2 Down / 1 Up

101

2 Down / 3 Up / 1 Up / Up / Down

102

Make 2 rows of chain stitches in a parallel fashion, then pass another thread through the inside of the chain stitches so they alternate.

2 Down / 3 Up / 1 Up

103

2 Down / 1 Up / 3 Up / 5 Up / 4 Down

Wrap the thread with a bead over the needle and press the bead with a finger to make it easier to pull the thread and fix the bead.

P.54 Line Stitch
Embroidery threads/beads used

97	Appleton double yarns 758 (red), 544 (lime green)/round bead 8/0 (3.0mm) 332 (red-purple), 557 (gold)
98	Appleton double yarns 758 (red), 544 (lime green)/round bead 8/0 (3.0mm) 264 (turquoise blue)
99	Appleton double yarns 758 (red), 564 (blue)/round bead 8/0 (3.0mm) 23 (aqua)
100	Appleton double yarns 758 (red)/round bead 8/0 (3.0mm) 557 (gold), 264 (turquoise blue)
101	Appleton double yarns 758 (red), 991 (white)/round bead 8/0 (3.0mm) 557 (gold)
102	Appleton double yarns 758 (red), 544 (lime green)/round bead 8/0 (3.0mm) 108 (green)
103	Appleton double yarns 758 (red)/round bead 8/0 (3.0mm) 264 (turquoise blue), 405 (red)

104

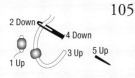
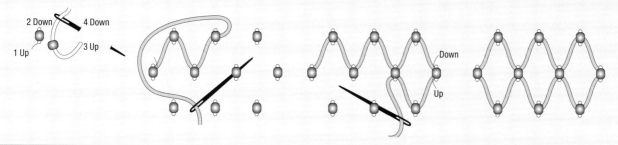

105

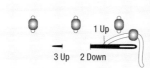

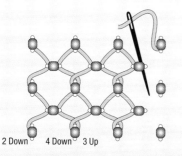

(170)

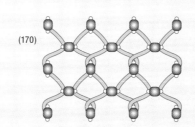

P.56 Filling Stitch
Embroidery threads/beads used

104 No.5 single yarn ECRU (natural undyed color), 747 (aqua), 807 (aqua), 517 (blue)/round bead 8/0 (3.0mm) 401 (white), 163 (blue), 170 (pale blue)

105 557 (gold), No.5 single yarn ECRU (natural undyed color), 807 (aqua), 518 (blue), 517 (blue)/round bead 8/0 (3.0mm) 401 (white), 163 (blue), 170 (pale blue), 557 (gold)

106 No.5 single yarn 747 (aqua), 807 (aqua), 518 (blue)/round bead 8/0 (3.0mm) 23 (blue), 180 (pale blue)

107 No.5 single yarn 747 (aqua), 807 (aqua), 517 (blue)/round bead 8/0 (3.0mm) 401 (white), 170 (pale blue), 23 (blue)

108 No.5 single yarn 747 (aqua), 807 (aqua), 518 (blue), 517 (blue)/round bead 8/0 (3.0mm) 163 (blue), 170 (pale blue), 401 (white), 23 (blue)

P.58 Interlaced Cross Stitch
Embroidery threads/beads used

109 Left: No.25 827 (aqua, double yarns), Diamant D168 (silver, single yarn)/round bead 11/0 (2.2mm) 558 (platinum)

Middle: No.25 827 (aqua, triple yarns), Diamant D168 (silver, double yarns)/round bead 11/0 (2.2mm) 558 (platinum)

Right: No.25 827 (aqua, triple yarns), Diamant D168 (silver, triple yarns)/round bead 11/0 (2.2mm) 558 (platinum)

110 Left: No.25 827 (aqua, triple yarns), Diamant D168 (silver, double yarns)/round bead 11/0 (2.2mm) 558 (platinum)

Middle: No.25 827 (aqua, double yarns), Diamant D168 (silver, single yarn)/round bead 11/0 (2.2mm) 558 (platinum)

Right: No.25 827 (aqua, triple yarns), Diamant D168 (silver, triple yarns)/round bead 11/0 (2.2mm) 558 (platinum)

111 Left: No.25 827 (aqua, triple yarns), Diamant D168 (silver, double yarns)/round bead 11/0 (2.2mm) 558 (platinum)

Middle: No.25 827 (aqua, double yarns), Diamant D168 (silver, single yarn)/round bead 11/0 (2.2mm) 558 (platinum)

Right: No.25 827 (aqua, triple yarns), Diamant D168 (silver, triple yarns)/round bead 11/0 (2.2mm) 558 (platinum)

112 No.25 827 (aqua, triple yarns), Diamant D168 (silver, double yarns)/round bead 11/0 (2.2mm) 558 (platinum)

106

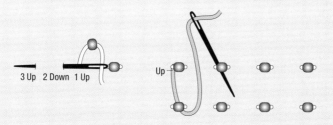
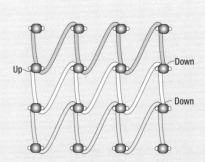

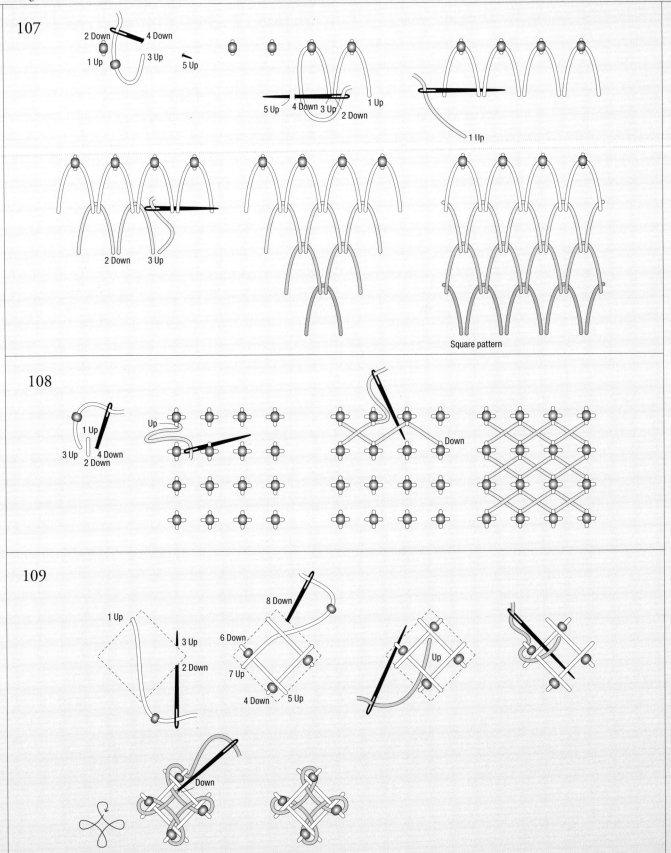

107

2 Down · 4 Down
1 Up · 3 Up · 5 Up

5 Up · 4 Down · 3 Up · 2 Down · 1 Up

1 Up

2 Down · 3 Up

Square pattern

108

1 Up
3 Up · 4 Down
2 Down

Up

Down

109

1 Up
3 Up
2 Down

8 Down
6 Down
7 Up
4 Down · 5 Up

Up

Down

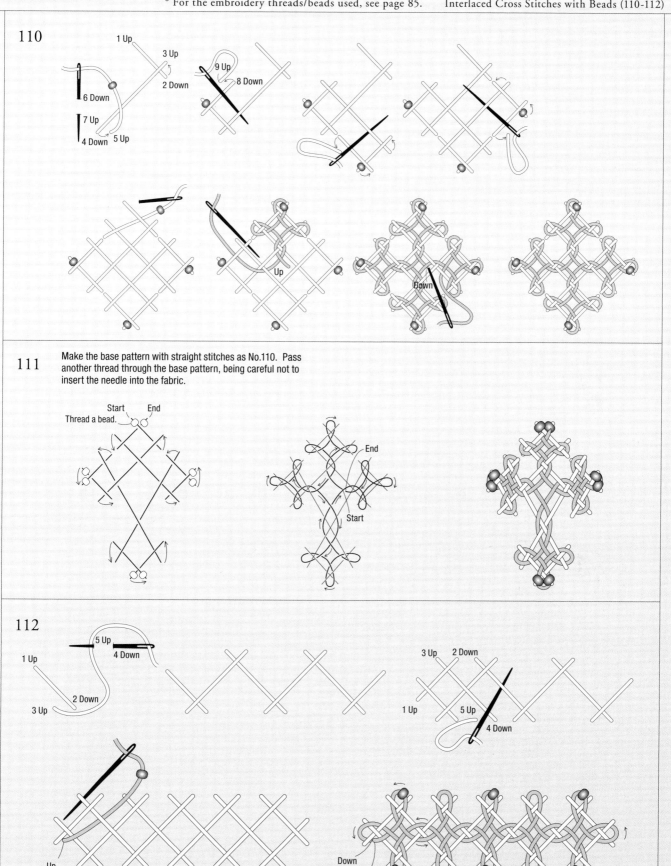

110

111 Make the base pattern with straight stitches as No.110. Pass another thread through the base pattern, being careful not to insert the needle into the fabric.

112

Authors' Profiles

C·R·K design

Graphic & craft designer: Chiaki Kitaya, Kaoru Emoto, Kuma Imamura, Yasuko Endo, Kumiko Yajima and Noriko Yoshiue. An unit of 6 designers with an infinite amount of creative energy dedicated to the handmade craft ideas is now actively engaged in a wide variety of work, from planning & production, book design and editing to direction and coordination for photo shoots! Books published include "The Beaded Edge: Inspired Designs for Crocheted Edgings and Trims," "The Beaded Edge 2," "Bead Embroidery Stitch Samples," "A Journy into Traditional Japanese Textiles" (published by Graphicsha). Many of their publications have been published all over the world.

Yasuko Endo

Upon graduating from the department of Apparel Design at Joshibi University of Art and Design Junior College, Yasuko Endo joined the planning department of an apparel manufacturer, and later turned freelance. Her main duty in C·R·K design is to make craft and home décor products. Awakened to the beauty of Japanese kimono and vintage fabrics, she now takes lessons in Japanese dressmaking techniques. Inspired by Japanese traditional handmade craft, she is now inventing embroidery design ideas suggesting the Iki (meaning chic in Japanese) of the Edo era.

Page 4 - Top-right boots: national flag motifs <stitch designs 37, 13, 40, 16, 19, 28>. For the materials, see page 74.

Page 5 - Top-left black cardigan: paisley motifs <stitch design 48>: for the materials, see page 31. Smaller paisley motifs <stitch design 44>: DMC No.25 4205 (reddish, double yarns), Diamant D3821 (gold, single yarn)/round bead 8/0 (3.0mm) 558 (platinum)/3mm-long bugle bead (332, red-purple)

Page 5 - Top-right linen handkerchief: sweets motifs <stitch design 3>: DMC No.25 676 (beige, triple yarns), 963 (pink, double yarns)/round bead 8/0 (3.0mm) 405 (red), 174 (orange), 402 (yellow), 105 (lime green)/round bead 11/0 (2.2mm) 332 (red-purple), 145 (pink)/6mm-long bugle bead 332 (red-purple). Checkered handkerchief: sweets motifs <stitch design 10> - Left: DMC No. 25 BLANC (white, double yarns), 962 (pink, double yarns)/round bead 8/0 (3.0mm) 121, 332 (red-purple)/3mm-long bugle bead 121 (white), 43 (aqua). Middle: DMC No. 25 BLANC (white, double yarns), 827 (aqua, double yarns)/ round bead 8/0 (3.0mm) 121 (white), 174 (orange), 105 (lime green), 405 (red)/ 3mm-long bugle bead 332 (red-purple), 43 (aqua). Right: DMC No. 25 BLANC (white, double yarns), 3822 (yellow, double yarns)/round bead 8/0 (3.0mm) 332 (red-purple), 174 (orange), 402 (yellow), 405 (red), 105 (lime green)/ 3mm-long bugle bead 102 (yellow), 121 (white)

Page 5: bottom-left dungaree shirt: ethnic costume motifs <stitch design 22, 23, 24>: for the materials, see pages 70 and 74.

Page 5: bottom-right black dress <stitch design 111>: DMC No. 25 827 (aqua, double yarns), Diamant D3821 (gold, double yarns)/2mm pearl 200 (white)

The linen shirt on page 1 is a sample piece from "Bead Embroidery Stitch Samples" published in 2012. Main materials used for the shirt are as follows. For the stitch design, refer to "Bead Embroidery Stitch Samples."

Linen shirt <stitch design 52>: DMC No. 25 3804 (pink, quadruple yarns), 334 (green, quadruple yarns)/round bead 8/0 (3.0mm) 558 (platinum), 332 (red-purple), <stitch design 37>: DMC No. 25 3843 (purple, triple yarns), round bead 8/0 (3.0mm) 252 (purple), 977 (purple), 31 (light pink), <stitch design 40>: DMC No. 25 915 (dark red, triple yarns)/round bead 8/0 (3.0mm) 31 (clear pink), 332 (red-purple)

Camisole: <stitch design 101>: DMC No.12 B5200 (white), No.8 B5200 (white) EDRU (natural undyed color)/round bead 8/0 (3.0mm) 106 (light pink), 123 (off-white)